Embodiment and Black Religion

Embodiment and Black Religion

Rethinking the Body in African American Religious Experience

CERCL Writing Collective

SHEFFIELD UK   BRISTOL CT

Published by Equinox Publishing Ltd.
UK: Office 415, The Workstation, 15 Paternoster Row, Sheffield, South Yorkshire S1 2BX
USA: ISD, 70 Enterprise Drive, Bristol, CT 06010

www.equinoxpub.com

First published 2017

© CERCL Writing Collective 2017

All rights reserved. No part of this publication may be reproduced or transmitted in any form or by any means, electronic or mechanical, including photocopying, recording or any information storage or retrieval system, without prior permission in writing from the publishers.

British Library Cataloguing-in-Publication Data

A catalogue record for this book is available from the British Library.

ISBN-13 978 1 78179 345 9 (hardback)
        978 1 78179 346 6 (paperback)

Library of Congress Cataloging-in-Publication Data

Names: CERCL Writing Collective, author.
Title: Embodiment and Black religion: rethinking the body in African American religious experience / CERCL Writing Collective.
Description: Bristol, CT: Equinox Publishing Ltd, 2017. | Includes bibliographical references and index.
Identifiers: LCCN 2016055124 (print) | LCCN 2016056569 (ebook) | ISBN 9781781793459 (hb) | ISBN 9781781793466 (pb) | ISBN 9781781795873 (ePDF)
Subjects: LCSH: African Americans—Religious life. | Human body—Religious aspects. | African American churches.
Classification: LCC BL625.2 .C47 2017 (print) | LCC BL625.2 (ebook) | DDC 204.408996073—dc23
LC record available at https://lccn.loc.gov/2016055124

Typeset by S.J.I. Services, New Delhi
Printed and bound by Lightning Source Inc. (La Vergne, TN), Lightning Source UK Ltd. (Milton Keynes), Lightning Source AU Pty. (Scoresby, Victoria).

Contents

Acknowledgements — vii

Introduction: Bodies *and* Religion — 1

Part One: Religion in Traditional Forms

1. "Heaven Knows No Color": Hybrid Bodies in Father Divine's Peace Mission Movement — 13

2. Arm, Leg, Leg, Arm, Head, This is God Body: The Body as a Site of Religious Expression in the Five Percenters — 32

Part Two: Cultural Production

3. Making Bodies with a Brush Stroke: African American Visual Art and the Re/constitution of Black Embodiment — 47

4. Unchained Bodies: Black Womanhood, Resistance, and Complex Subjectivity in Black Literature — 59

5. It Was Written on Her Face: Religion and Black Women's Embodied Emotion in Film — 71

6. "School Daze": Embodiment and Meaning-making in Black Greek Letter Organizations — 82

Part Three: Religion in Everyday Life

7. Hoodies and Headwraps: Everyday Religion and the Dressing of Black Bodies — 97

8	Gathering around the Table: Food Practices and Religious Meaning	117
9	Every-Body's Truth: The New Genetics of Race and the Quest for Complex Subjectivity	125
	Epilogue	137
	Bibliography	139
	Index	147

Acknowledgements

The motivation for this project originates from a joint venture between Rice University's Center for Engaged Research and Collaborative Learning (CERCL) and the University of Kent.

Beginning in 2012, Dr. Anthony B. Pinn, Agnes Cullen Arnold Professor of Humanities and Professor of Religious Studies at Rice University, and Dr. Gordon Lynch, Michael Ramsey Professor of Modern Theology at the University of Kent—along with some of their graduate students—organized and participated in several workshops, funded by Rice, in both Houston (USA) and Canterbury (UK). During these workshops, they discussed various topics related to the study of religion and embodiment. *Embodiment and Black Religion* is one of the outcomes of this collaboration. The CERCL Writing Collective would like to acknowledge the following for their contributions that helped to inform this project and make it possible: Anthony Pinn, Gordon Lynch, David Morgan, Emily Falconer, Melissa Caldwell, Ann Strhan, Yvette Taylor Shard, Ward Blanton, Rachel Hanemann, Chris Shilling, Aundrea Matthews, Jonathan Chism, Terri Laws, Christopher Driscoll, Maya Reine, University of Kent, Canterbury Cathedral, and Rice University. We also would like to acknowledge the Rice University Faculty Initiative Fund for generous support for this project. Finally, we would like to thank Dr. Christopher Stewart, Yvette Calm, and the Peace Mission Movement for permission to reprint the images contained in this volume.

Introduction: Bodies *and* Religion

Bodies *and* religion. These are two terms whose referential content spans space and time in ways that fold in on themselves. What we name in this text is a locus of relation, a constellation of varying conceptual, political, theological and scientific engagement between religion and the body. The "and" names a nexus between those two entities and we have set ourselves the task of tracing its contours and following its movement. As we will show, the very meaning of the "and" takes us to places we hadn't expected to go: from black vegans to Black Greek Letter Organizations (BGLOs), from genetics to dress, and from Ava DuVernay to Jean-Michel Basquiat. Our attempt to track this nexus has taken us beyond the well-worn path of trying to understand the meaning of the body in what are commonly called "religious traditions". While we certainly turn to movements and organizations that could be called "religions" or "religious traditions", our search has taken us past these organizations. So, while we might not want to pin the "body" or "religion" down as concrete, static entities, it is possible—and indeed, from our perspective, it becomes necessary—to speak of both religion and bodies in dynamic and processual ways. One such way is to understand religion and bodies as operating in tandem. Far from speaking of religion and bodies as two juxtaposed entities forced together by way of conjunctive connection, they both are malleable enough to work with each other. In this way, the compatibility of bodies with religion—and vice versa—can be explored, by understanding the body as the *"space" wherein meaning is made, developed and maintained*, while understanding religion *as the very effort to make, develop and maintain (if necessary) certain structures of meaning*. In this regard, we find much use in Anthony Pinn's theory of religion as the quest for complex subjectivity.

THE QUEST FOR COMPLEX SUBJECTIVITY

By "the quest for complex subjectivity", Pinn names the process of seeking greater life meaning—or, as he has often put it, the process of figuring out "who, what, when, where, and why we are". The quest for complex subjectivity, then, names a process and not a tradition—although traditions (such as humanism, the Nation of Islam, and African American Christian churches) stand as historical manifestations of this particular process. Pinn's theory invokes two areas of human thought and engagement: ontology and identity. With regard to ontology, the quest emerges out of a very specific context: the myriad reductions of human beings to historical objects. In *Terror and Triumph* (2003), Pinn focuses specifically on the historical realities of the auction block and the lynching tree, two sites in which black women and men were reified into objects. Pinn refers to these processes of historical reification and objectification as "rituals of reference": the repeated and systematic process of depriving one of one's humanity in and through their very bodies. What happens is an ontological deprivation, as the complexity of one's being is sapped from him or her through barter and sale or through mutilation and extralegal killing.

But if these rituals of reference constitute an ontological assault, they also raise a question concerning identity. In the face of a sale or lynching, black slaves asked themselves who and what they were in relation to this world that would enslave, sell, mutilate and murder them. This question of identity—of who and what one is—therefore becomes the quintessentially religious question, precisely because it emerges out of a context wherein one's personal orientation and relationship to the world has been wholly altered. In *Terror and Triumph*, one can hear the echoes of Charles Long's definition of religion as "orientation in the ultimate sense" (Long 1986, 7) but this time, the question of "orientation" is also a question of meaning—not the interpretation of meaning (as Long might attest), but rather the construction and maintenance of this meaning. What religion is, then, is the process of trying to beat back the baggage of history; it is our attempt to resist whatever efforts might be made to turn us into historical objects. As human beings, we want *more*; and it is this yearning for more, this push for a greater and more meaningful life, that is the spring of religion and religious experience.

The quest for complex subjectivity names a process that can occur within the context of art galleries, coffee shops and barbershops, as well as—and we will demonstrate that here—literary novels, movies, food choices, and the tracing of one's ancestry. As an open-ended process, the quest for complex subjectivity is not any of these spaces, places or practices, but rather the source of these things. Religion as quest, per Pinn, is more fundamental and more expansive than any of these realities; it is our way of pushing for a greater sense of self in relation to others and the world within which we find ourselves.

THE COMPOUND BODY

This formulation of religion prompted Pinn to have to address the question of the body. If the quest for complex subjectivity is motivated by the ontological and existential attacks and constraints on the body, then how might we speak of these bodies? While Pinn certainly already provides some clues in *Terror and Triumph*, thereby building on Michel Foucault and Mary Douglas, he expanded on this in his later text *Embodiment and the New Shape of Black Theological Thought* (2010). In *Embodiment*, he again draws on Foucault—among a host of other thinkers—to develop the compound body of which we spoke above.

For Pinn, the body has two dimensions: discursive and biochemical. The discursive dimension refers to the many ways that social constructs come to define, frame, and often trap the body. This discursive reality can range from the most general of identity categories such as race, gender and sexuality, to more specific meanings coded on the bases of these more general categories. In this discursive dimension, representations, stereotypes, analyses, and depictions of bodies—as well as the treatment resulting from these various rays of this discursive dimension—bear down upon the second dimension of the body (the biochemical dimension) in order to make it legible and, in many cases, subject it or render it docile. The biochemical dimension is that material reality to which certain scientific analyses alert us. This dimension includes the cells, neurons, synapses, bones, muscles and tissue that compose the material body, allowing it to move, feel and sense the world. This biochemical dimension alerts us to the fact that we are living, breathing, feeling beings who are born, grow, live, decay, and then die.

When thought of as a complex but continuous unit, this compound body makes it possible for us to consider the complexity of human life, and the various constraints and conditioned freedoms we experience as physical beings. And this compound body is compatible with the quest for complex subjectivity because it attends to the ontological and existential constraints placed upon us via our bodies, as well as our perpetual yearning (as beings who are born, live, have relationships, and die) for a greater and better sense of self in relation to others and the world within which we find ourselves.

To be sure, our argument is particularly grounded in Pinn's understanding of religion as an embodied quest for complex subjectivity. But if his theory speaks to religion, this project picks up where he left off by giving careful consideration to religion's forms.

More specifically, in addressing particular case studies that reflect the variety of ways in which bodies are entangled and engaged in struggles for life meaning, we argue that African American religion takes on various forms, including modes of cultural production as well as mundane, everyday rituals and practices. We find Pinn's work on the body and religion a good starting point—but again, it is merely a starting point.

Our goal in this text is to speak to how religion and bodies are shifted, expanded and deconstructed when they are considered in tandem. Our suggestion is that, above anything else, this relationship reveals our desire or yearning for expansive lives—in particular as related to African Americans living in the United States.

CHAPTER OVERVIEW

Religion and bodies shift, and we trace these shifts and movements throughout three sections. The chapters bear the mark of these two framings—religion and bodies—but do not always explicitly reference them.

The chapters in "Part One: Religion in Traditional Forms" look at two black religious traditions, the Peace Mission movement and the Nation of Gods and Earths (Five Percenters). These chapters argue theoretical attention to the body in more traditional forms of religion pushes discussion beyond dogma, doctrine and written texts. The first chapter, "Heaven Knows No Color: Hybrid Bodies in Father Divine's Peace Mission Movement", suggests that several pictures of Mother and Father Divine, shot during their wedding day and artificially altered in such a way that both seem to have a similar, off-white skin color, should be understood as a performance that aims at creating a new racialized identity of hybridity. This argument puts bodies at the center of Father Divine's work and demonstrates that a turn towards bodies—through these images—permits a new understanding of his post-racial imaginaries. The second chapter, "Arm, Leg, Leg, Arm, Head, this is God Body", suggests the body is central to, in and for Five Percenters religion—given that Five Percenters consider the black body proof of God's existence and central to gaining what is known in the movement as "knowledge of self". Chapters 1 and 2 raise questions about where and when we find religion and bodies colliding—images, as is the case with Father Divine, or in Five Percenter rap lyrics and "ciphers".

If the body is a principal site through which the black religious quest happens, then this warrants a broader examination of black religion beyond traditional and institutional forms of religious practice. In Part Two, we take up depictions, representations and engagements with the body in African American cultural production, including visual art, literature, film and certain practices within Black Greek Letter Organizations. In so doing, we offer a more expansive account of black religion by arguing that modes of cultural production "house" the religious quest for complex subjectivity. We begin by building a case for our argument in Chapter 3, "Making Bodies with a Brush Stroke: African American Visual Art and the Re/constitution of Black Embodiment". Through an analysis of Jean Michel Basquiat's artwork, we point to the function of visual art by arguing that Basquiat's images of bodies without organs, or deconstructed bodies, reflect an understanding of the body that is fluid, undefined, and ever-changing. Basquiat's paintings thus "re-present" black bodies and black life beyond fixed, stereotypical depictions. We continue to interrogate the religious significance of creative reconstructions of the black body through cultural production by turning to two literary depictions of black women in Chapter 4, "Unchained Bodies: Black Womanhood, Resistance, and Complex Subjectivity in Black Literature". Here, we posit that the female protagonists in Toni Morrison's *Beloved* and Octavia Butler's *Wild Seed* assume "gender fluid" identities that subvert patriarchal and white supremacist constructions of black women's bodies. In Chapter 5, "It Was Written on Her Face: Religion and Black Women's Embodied Emotion in Film", we maintain our specific focus on depictions of black women's bodies, although from a slightly different angle. That is, while our larger emphasis in Chapter 4 is the religious significance of black women's resistance to demeaning discursive notions of black women's bodies, our focus in Chapter 5 is more on the material body. In turning attention to Ava DuVernay's silent short film, *The Door*, we trace the ways in which the quest for complex subjectivity plays out through the embodied emotions displayed by the black women characters in the film. More specifically, we argue that DuVernay's cinematic emphasis on their subtle facial expressions and bodily movements produces visual renderings of black women with emotional depth and dimensionality that eludes strict lines of representational categorization. Finally, we conclude our second section in Chapter 6, "'School Daze': Embodiment and Meaning-making in Black Greek Letter Organizations", by giving critical consideration to how black religion as the quest for complex subjectivity is worked out in the context of community and social traditions. In particular, we argue that the embodied practices of "branding" and "stepping" in Black Greek Letter Organizations (BGLOs) make these social spaces analogous to religious institutions, such that they signify processes of identity construction and meaning-making among their members, especially in the larger context of discrimination and limited life options often experienced by black college students. In each of these chapters, we find ourselves capturing and captured by the relation between bodies and religion as it relates to the construction and maintenance of meaning.

While our second section claims that centralizing the body expands the category of religion in important ways, section three furthers the argument by positing that religious meaning can also be found in the mundane, everyday aspects of embodied life. The three chapters in this section demonstrate that specific bodily engagements such as dress and fashion, eating, and racial genetics can be sites of meaning-making, particularly when done in the context of community. Using the events and controversies surrounding Trayvon Martin, Rachel Dolezal and Sarah Valentine as case studies, Chapter 7, "Hoodies and Headwraps: Everyday Religion and the Dressing of Black Bodies", argues that dress and fashion are sites for both restrictive, discursive constructions of black embodiment as well as expressions of the quest for complex subjectivity. Through Frantz Fanon's understanding of the "historico-racial" schema that "fixes" bodies within an array of stereotypes and myths, this chapter begins by showing how fashion and dress can produce limited and/or dehumanizing understandings of identity, subjectivity and embodiment. We then demonstrate how individual constructions of "fashion subjectivity" constitute an embodied push for meaning and more expansive ontological possibilities. From this chapter we move to a discussion of the practice of eating as being religiously informed. Chapter 8, "Gathering around the Table: Food Practices and Religious Meaning" argues that black veganism can be understood as a form of religious meaning-making. Black vegans' food practices and belief systems are seen as a religious form of resisting the legacy of slavery that equated enslaved Africans with animals. By abstaining from eating animal products, black vegans see themselves as refusing the system that once enslaved them and continues to objectify and dehumanize black bodies. While the first two chapters in this section address specific everyday practices moving from what we put on our bodies to what we put into them, the final chapter looks to the body's innermost reality. Chapter 9, "Every-Body's Truth: The New Genetics of Race and the Quest for Complex Subjectivity", argues that contemporary understandings of racial genetics and its links to identity construction can function as part of a stronger push for an expanded sense of meaning. Looking at the practice of African American "ancestor tracing", this chapter shows that knowledge of the body at the genetic level—which stands as an expansion of the biochemical dimension of the compound body—provides an occasion for experiencing the *mysterium tremendum*.

CONCLUDING THOUGHTS

This text demonstrates a collective journey. We sought to write a book that would push past contemporary approaches to black religion. By doing so, we hope to offer a corrective to and expand current scholarship on religion and embodiment, particularly in African American Religious Studies, in (at least) three important ways. First, the chapters in this book go beyond an understanding of black religion as the "Black Church" and underscore the variety of African American religious experiences, which pertain to both marginal religious traditions as well as non-traditional forms of religion. Unlike recent scholarship on black religion and the body, our journey is not a Christian theological treatment, framing the body in relation to the development of Christian doctrine. Second, our sustained and rigorous attention to theories of the body allows for a more robust understanding of what the body is, and moves beyond the implicit understandings of the body as solely discursive that are prevalent in the field.[1] Third, our approach is interdisciplinary. While grounded in Religious Studies, this book puts various theories and methodologies—from the social sciences to philosophy, and from visual studies to literary studies—in conversation with the religious experiences of African Americans.[2]

From orientations/traditions, to cultural production, to the mundane practices of sartorial presentation, vegan lifestyles, and genetic ancestry tracing, our search took us to places that otherwise may have been left unexplored. In this way, *Embodiment and Black Religion* stands as an offering and a prompt: it is our theoretical offering to think critically about the expansive and often unexplored areas of embodiment and religion. But more than this, it is a collective prodding to the field of African American religious studies to continue along this journey, to rethink how and where religion might be found—especially when it is explored in tandem with the bodies that express, frame and articulate it in their daily movements, discursive (re)presentations and physical transformations.

ONE LAST CONSIDERATION

The question of the relationship between bodies and religion is not merely relegated to the arena of the academic. Religion and bodies, bodies and religion, are constantly intervening in our individual and collective lives. For instance, when we think of African Americans in the United States, we need not go much further than Missouri police officer Darren Wilson labeling Michael Brown "an angry demon" or Dylann Roof murdering nine black women and men in a South Carolina church to realize how the very presence of black bodies is often perceived as constituting a dangerous threat that must be neutralized or eliminated. In one scene, a black body was coded in the terminology of the demonic, literally producing a theological justification for murder; in the other, black bodies were in a traditionally religious space that afforded them no solace from the negative meanings encoded in their very flesh. In both events we can hear the echoes of Charles Long's work in that these black bodies were *signified*, given names that are "at the same time an objectification through categories and concepts of those realities which appear as novel and 'other' to the cultures of conquest" (Long 1986, 4). Whether the black body is coded as a demon or blamed for the failure of one's country and the sexual assault of white women, throughout African American history, we see religion and bodies in a perpetual "dance" of sorts.

But the relationship between religion and black bodies isn't all tragedy. From Beyoncé's self-presentation as a Yoruba goddess in her music videos to the beauty of a hymn sung by a soloist in a black Christian church on Sunday; from the collective masses of bodies who would gather in the streets in protest, to the humanist celebration of the mundane through walks in the park; from the embodied freedom made possible through break dancing, to the high self-esteem afforded one by how he or she dresses—in these and countless other cases, we find times where bodies and religion are dancing with each other in rhythm, to the same tune and on the same beat. In the history of African American life in the United States, we see that the relationship between bodies and religion is complex, open-ended, and perpetually changing.

A WORD ON PROCESS

This book represents an experiment with communication of ideas across difference—a wrestling with the presentation of voice and exchange. In a word, it is a co-authored volume in which each member of the CERCL collaborative—Anthony Pinn, Jessica Davenport, Mark DeYoung, Justine Bakker, Jason Jeffries, Biko Gray, Shardé Chapman, Cleve Tinsley and David Kline—is responsible for the initial drafting of a chapter. Presenting this draft is not the end of the process; rather, it marks the start of an exchange defined by a desire to push the nature and scope of collaboration.

Once written, each chapter was reviewed and revised in light of group conversation—so as to trouble a sense of isolated ownership of the ideas, and to promote appreciation for refinement of ideas through conversation. We have tried to highlight the collective voice marked by intellectual cooperation on religion and bodies. Something of the first author remains present, but the final version of each chapter entails that first author in conversation with the other members of the collective. This is not to suggest there is full agreement on all of the ideas present, but such agreement is not the point. Rather, the goal was to promote an organic "reworking" that marked the ability to speak together, while maintaining the importance of disagreement. The process undertaken in this book, as well as in our first effort (*Breaking Bread, Breaking Beats: Churches and Hip-Hop—A Basic Guide to Key Issues*, 2014), is still in development and shows a variety of shortcomings to be sure. Still, it is an important effort to privilege robust collaboration within the production of scholarship. What undergirds both our agreements and disagreements is a shared concern with investigation of religion and bodies within the framework of African American religious studies. This, of course, does not constitute the final word on this subject. Rather, we hope it will spark ongoing consideration of the topic and in the process expand the reach and content of African American religious studies.

NOTES

1 Recent examples include Copeland (2008), Turman (2014), Douglas (1999; 2005) and Townes (2006)—all of whom provide largely discursive framings of the body through Christian discourse. Copeland's *Enfleshing Freedom* (2008) recasts the body—particularly the broken bodies of black women—as new opportunities for eucharistic celebration. Drawing a strong parallel between the treatment of Jesus' body and the daily lives of women of color across the world,

Copeland makes a strong case for thinking about black women's bodies as the site for individual and collective freedom. Turman's *Toward a Womanist Ethic of Incarnation* (2014) provides a similar conclusion—namely, she recasts black women's bodies in a christological role—except her work is framed less around the Eucharist than it is about the composition of the body, particularly the bodies of black women and Jesus. Discussing the early church hearings about the nature of Jesus' existence (that is, his unique existence as a divine/human entity), Turman argues that Jesus was constantly navigating between two natures. In other words, he was *mediating* between what happened *to* him as a human being and what was happening *in* him as a divine entity. Drawing from Marcia Y. Riggs's mediating ethic, she argues that black women also have to navigate/mediate between what happens *to* them as black women who are often oppressed by manifold structures, as well as what happens *in* them as human beings framed in the image of God. Drawing on her experience as a dancer, she discusses how the choreographed bodily movements of black women show how they mediate between these two realities, tracing how that movement speaks to an embodied mediation of these two realities—and a push against them. In *Sexuality and the Black Church* (1999) and *What's Faith Got to Do with It* (2005), Douglas provides multiple analyses of the body, but she ultimately argues, in both texts, for an understanding of the body as an expression of the *imago dei*. Whether it is in how we think of our sexuality—that is, the ways in which we express our love in embodied terms—or how we think of the body more generally, Douglas provides significant theological resources for pushing against the dominant Christian disavowal of the body—and more specifically bodies of color. And lastly, Townes's *Womanist Ethics and the Cultural Production of Evil* (2006) speaks about stereotypical representations of black women; these representations frame black women's bodies in ways that allow for societies and cultures to visit all kinds of devastation on black women.

In all four of these treatments, we find discursive representations of black bodies—particularly black women's bodies. We are made acutely aware of how various discourses—be they theological, scientific, political or cultural—frame black bodies and condition their movement throughout the world. But this discursive approach narrowly speaks to the body in largely Christian terms, and it also provides little analysis of *how* the body experiences the world, that is, how it moves through the world as a flesh-and-blood entity. This volume seeks to take the body's movement more seriously, moving away from Christian framings while appreciating the body's involvement in and interaction with the religious.

2 In this regard, we are heavily influenced by thinkers such as Charles Long, whose *Significations* (1986) is largely interdisciplinary, drawing from various methods to develop a complex hermeneutical approach to the study of religion. Other thinkers such as Chireau (2003) provide a sharp critique of the distinction between "religion" and "magic" by paying close attention to African American religious cultures. Although we do not fully share their theoretical dispositions, we acknowledge that our work is influenced by attempts like these—attempts to think about religion in as many ways as possible.

Part One

Religion in Traditional Forms

Chapter One

"Heaven Knows No Color": Hybrid Bodies in Father Divine's Peace Mission Movement

On April 29, 1946, Edna Rose Ritchings, a young white woman from Vancouver, Canada, traveled to Washington DC to marry a black man. At a time when interracial marriages were still forbidden in many US states, the wedding was in and of itself highly scandalous, but the identity of the man she was about to marry was perhaps even more astonishing. The groom, known to his followers as Father Divine, was literally believed to be God in a body. It is said that Ms. Ritchings, when she was one of his secretaries, even proposed to Father Divine with the words: "I want to marry YOU because I know YOU are GOD" (Peace Mission Movement [no date, a], emphasis original).

Father Divine was the founder and leader of the Peace Mission Movement, an interracial religious movement founded in the 1920s that adhered to a strict moral code and practiced celibacy. The wedding, which epitomized the union of "God and man", was therefore to be "in name only"—that is, not physically consummated. Mother Divine, as Ms. Ritchings came to be known, was thought to be a "spotless virgin bride" and believed to be a "reincarnation" of that other, much more famous virgin, Mary (F. Divine 1976, 23). The wedding served, in the words of Divine, as a "visualization" of the holiness of Christ and the virginity of Mary, or, the "perfection of humanity" (M. Divine 1982, 55). In other words, this wedding, for Divine, actualized or materialized—in his terminology, "visualized"—the Kingdom of God on Earth. As further evidence of the importance of this spiritual wedding, we should note that the year 1946 would, from then on, be conceived as "year one" in the Peace Mission Movement. The date April 29, in turn, became an "International, Interracial, Universal Holiday" (M. Divine 1982; Peace Mission Movement [no date, a]).

Following the ceremony, the newlywed couple distributed a set of photographs, which circulated widely among followers, were published in *New Day*, the movement's newspaper, and continue to decorate the walls of Peace Mission Movement premises, implying their importance (Primiano 2009, 107; Satter 1996, 64). While photography has always been important to the Peace Mission Movement (Primiano 2015), these particular images are distinct in an important way. The black-and-white photos of the interracial couple were artificially painted so that the skin color of husband and wife would match. That is, specially assigned "angels" (as followers of Divine are known) rendered Father Divine's complexion lighter, and Mother Divine's complexion darker, resulting in a somewhat unified, off-white or grayish complexion for both (see Figure 1). In the 1950s, the Peace Mission Movement disseminated an additional set of images, a set of formal portraits in color, in which Father and Mother Divine are cast in the same shade of faded orange (see Figure 2).[1]

Divine never commented on these images himself, but there has been some scholarly discussion around them. Leonard Primiano (2009), for instance, refers to the images as an example of Divine's "deracialized perspective" (107). Beryl Satter, with a somewhat different emphasis, situates the photos within the context of a change in Divine's teachings in the 1950s, which constituted a "reshaping" of his life and image in accordance with more "mainstream" white American ideals and culture. For instance, she notes that whereas Divine initially had a rather subversive take on gender roles by proposing gender equality, from the 1950s on he appears to have accepted the gender norms of white America (Satter 1996, 64). Hence, for her, the photos should be taken as part of this somewhat unexpected move towards an embrace of white America. Satter fails to note, however, that Divine was not only depicted as "lighter", but his wife also as "darker", which would seem to be rather out of step with "mainstream" (that is, white) American ideals.

We suggest a different framework. As these altered photographs depict an interracial couple who will purportedly actualize the Kingdom of God through their *celibate* marriage, we will place the artificially painted bodies first and foremost in the context of Divine's teachings on celibacy. In doing so, a different interpretation emerges: these photos, or, more specifically, the bodies depicted in these images, are *not* an example of Divine's "deracialized" perspective. Neither should they primarily be understood as part of a push towards mainstream American ideals. To the contrary, we contend they portray Divine's attempt to put forth a new racialized identity, that of hybridity. As will become evident, we use the notion of hybridity

"Heaven Knows No Color" 15

Figure 1. Mother and Father Divine. Photo taken in garden of Peace Mission Movement's Tarrytown Estate, New York. Courtesy of the Peace Mission Movement, Woodmont Estate, Gladwyne, Pennsylvania

Figure 2. Mother and Father Divine. Composite portrait. Courtesy of the Peace Mission Movement, Woodmont Estate, Gladwyne, Pennsylvania

to denote both the racial understanding of the term—in the sense of their unified skin coloration—as well as a merging between the human and the divine.[2]

For the purposes of this chapter, the photos are thus important to the extent that they seem to depict hybrid bodies as the epitome of an interracial America.[3] Turning our attention to bodies, more specifically to the bodies in these images, helps us to understand that Divine did not merely push for a post-racial society. Indeed, it is our contention that in, with, and through these photos, he also imagined and visualized a new, hybrid race. Understood and analyzed within the context of his teachings on celibacy and amalgamation, these artificially painted bodies thus allow us to formulate a new perspective on Divine's ideas about post-racial America.[4]

While these images should be understood as existing in the same register as Divine's teachings on a post-racial community and society and the role of celibacy in fashioning a new world and people, the images also tell us something more, something beyond mere words, in terms of how we look at and read bodies. Thus, whereas most research has concentrated more on the written or spoken practices and aspects of Divine's push for race-neutrality—such as his resistance to the use of "black" and "white" in favor of "dark complexion" and "light complexion"—this chapter will interrogate how such discourses were visualized. In doing so, we will also shift the conversation from a focus on "interracial" and "race-neutral" to "hybrid" bodies, as Divine and his followers embodied the idea of race-neutrality through performances that culminated in positing precisely the hybrid body as the "perfection of humanity". These bodies tell us something in addition to written or spoken text and doctrine: whereas Divine often spoke in rather vague terms about a post-racial community, society and America, they offer us a much more grounded idea of the visual aspects of such thinking.

AGAINST RACE, TOWARDS THE "POST-RACIAL"

Born as George Baker,[5] Father Divine (1879–1965) was perhaps most famous for his weekly Holy Communion Banquets, where all who were interested, black or white, followers or passers-by, could join in for a sermon and a free meal. In the 1930s, at the apex of Divine's religious leadership, thousands (scholars estimate as many as 50,000) were served each week (Watts 1992, 88, 122). Divine also had thousands of "core" followers—predominantly African American women (Satter 1996, 45, 68).[6] While he claimed to be "God in a body", he instructed these followers to strive for divine status as well, as he maintained that God could theoretically dwell in anyone. As observed by Jill Watts (1992) and R. Marie Griffith (2001), such ideas were grounded in New Thought, a label first used in 1889 to refer to a scattered and syncretic movement that evolved in the 1840s in New England from the teachings of Phineas Parkhurst Quimby (1802–1886). Often described as a kind of "self-help psychology", New Thought was based on the idea that one could create his or her own personal reality solely by harnessing the power of thought. New Thought became popular in the late nineteenth and early twentieth century and comprised a diverse set of religious and philosophical ideas culled from liberal Protestantism, spiritualism, mesmerism, rosicrucianism, and transcendentalism. This multiplicity of sources allowed for its broad appeal to a wide range of (African) Americans.

Immersed in New Thought ideas about positive thinking and the creative power of thought, Father Divine was convinced that the nature of reality was based upon ideas. He implied that "negative thinking" materialized or "visualized" as a detrimental reality, while positive thinking would result in favorable situations. Divine considered race and racism the offshoot of such negative thinking. Thus, he would claim that racial terms carried "the GERMS of SEGREGATION and DISCRIMINATION and the very germ of LOWRATION by the saying of such terms unconsciously" (F. Divine, 1945, cited in Satter 1996, 53, emphasis in original). Put simply, racism could be eradicated once and for all, if folks would simply stop using racial and ethnic slurs.[7] For Divine, race had no grounding in, and should not leave its mark on, the real world. Shedding light on the more practical implications of such "progressive" thinking, scholars often highlight that black and white "angels" lived together in communes, refused to verbally acknowledge race and racial difference and made sure that black and white diners were seated in an alternating pattern during Divine's famous banquets (Satter 1996, 44, 64–5; Watts 1992, 89–90; Primiano 2009, 107). The latter practice indicates, of course, that despite Father Divine's claims, race was, in the Peace Mission Movement, not of diminished importance.

Scholars have understood these practices as part of Divine's push for a more race-neutral or even proto-post-racial America. The images that are central to this chapter could be seen as part of this effort. As noted above, Beryl Satter regards Divine's marriage to a white woman, and the artificial alteration of the photos of the couple, as signs of Divine's emphasis on white American culture and his wish to transcend, in particular, his African roots. As evidence for this claim, Satter cites a statement that appeared frequently during the 1950s in *The New Day*, the Peace Mission's newspaper, in which Divine pressed: "I do NOT represent races, creeds or colors. Therefore I AM NOT what you think or take me to be. I AM NOT a N...o and I AM NOT representing any such thing as the N...o or the C... race. [...] I AM a REAL, TRUE AMERICAN ONE HUNDRED PERCENT" (F. Divine, 1953, cited in Satter, 1996, 64, emphasis original).

According to Satter, Divine's patriotism was primarily ignited by the outbreak of World War II, which he seemed to understand as a battle between racists and segregationists, on the one hand, and a peaceful planet Earth united under a one-world government and spearheaded by the United States, on the other hand. In an effort to promote this more idyllic, perhaps even utopian, view of the world, Divine supported the war and began to promote a brand of American nationalism among his "angels". Perceived as the (future) leader of a regime that was to eradicate all national, ethnic, and racial differences, America was now understood as the ideal of and location for the future Kingdom of God on earth (Satter 1996, 62; see also Watts 1992, 171).

Satter's argument that Divine, following World War II, embraced a curious form of patriotism—and that he indeed did so while he had once proudly expressed that he was not an American—is convincing, as is her case that Divine sought to transcend his black identity. Yet, the fact that "angels", during the heydays of Divine's patriotism, artificially reconstructed an image of Divine and his wife to portray a unified complexion could indicate that Divine did not attempt to secure this united and amalgamated world solely through the creation of interracial communities. That is, the images seem to suggest that Divine regarded the hybrid body— photographically rendered as off-white or faded orange—as the embodiment of the future ideals and reality of a "united" and "amalgamated" America.

CELIBACY AND THE "PERFECTION OF HUMANITY"

To be sure, the images that are discussed in this chapter are certainly not the only photographs of Mother and Father Divine that were available and known. In fact, in most of the available photos the color of their skin is natural and unaltered. However, in contrast to the bulk of the photographic archive of the movement, the images that are central to this chapter are altered and, according to Primiano (2009, 107) "flooded" the Peace Mission premises. And while we are more interested in the fact that the bodies depicted in these images were artificially painted than in offering a thick description of the pictures as such, it is also important to note that the images depict a celebration of the marriage between Father Divine and his young "spotless" bride. Divine's followers did not artificially alter each and every photo, but instead chose to modify—and subsequently distribute and publish—precisely those pictures that were meant to capture and freeze the visualization of the "perfection of humanity"—that is, his marriage to his "Spotless Virgin" bride. Precisely this piece of information, seemingly overlooked by other scholars, is significant if we want to understand the gravity and weight of these particular images. A turn towards Divine's teachings on celibacy, then, will help us to understand why these particular images are significant. We suggest that precisely because these photographs (re)present the perfection of humanity, they could be said to (re)present the kind of bodies that could or should inhabit the Kingdom of God. A turn towards the images, instead of focusing solely on writings and speeches, shows that Divine's teachings on celibacy are, albeit implicitly, part of his post-racial imaginaries.

The source of Divine's ideas on celibacy is not entirely clear. Since both Griffith (2001, 142) and Satter (1996, 54–5) demonstrate that many New Thought thinkers were celibate, it may be tempting to conclude that the practice found its way to Divine's theology and practice via that route. It is, however, also possible that Divine took an interest in celibacy during his youth, when he became familiar with celibate Catholic nuns and priests (Griffith 2001, 142; Kahan 2009, 53). In any case, it is clear that sexual abstinence was of utmost importance for the Peace Mission Movement. Living a celibate life was, for Divine, an absolute necessity in order to establish the Kingdom of God on earth, because celibacy equals virtue, and only in "innocence and purity" one can behold "God and HIS kingdom" (M. Divine 1982, 47).[8] The Peace Mission Movement's sexually segregated communes were believed to exemplify the living reality of heaven on earth. Divine was convinced that "self-denial" was the best way to partake in God's consciousness and allowed followers to become as close as possible to unity with the divine. Furthermore, Divine claimed that only those who practiced celibacy would ultimately be redeemed (F. Divine 1974a, 3). Marcus Garvey, who was one of Divine's most vocal opponents in the 1930s, reasoned differently. For Garvey, Divine's practice of celibacy would not lead to redemption for blacks, but to "the complete extermination of the Negro race" (Garvey 1936, cited in Satter 1996, 43).

The emphasis on, and relationship between, Divine's divinity, celibacy, virginity, and the Kingdom of God is further expressed in the three Divinite orders that were established between 1938 and 1941: the Rosebuds, the

Crusaders, and the Lily-buds. The Crusaders and the Rosebuds consisted of virgins, men and women respectively, "who pattern their lives after the Virginity of Mary and the Holiness of Jesus" (M. Divine 1982, 32). The relationship between Divine as redeemer of mankind and the virginity of the Rosebuds was constantly emphasized. According to Divine, only virgins were "pure and clean, incorruptible and undefiled" (F. Divine 1974a, 3).

Whereas Benjamin Kahan (2009) has argued that Divine's commitment to celibacy refashioned ideas about black sexuality, thereby broadening its possibilities, one could also argue, by contrast, that this simply reinforced the attempts of black middle-class respectability politics to police ostensibly raucous promiscuity among black people. Moreover, the practice of celibacy left unchanged the persistent fear of anti-miscegenation by insisting that the co-habitation of black and white should not produce (mixed-race) offspring.

The Peace Mission Movement taught that only virgins could be transformed and saved by Divine, as *his* body serves as the source of salvation, redemption and change. Divine even claimed to have the ability to restore the virginity of the followers who had engaged in sexual intercourse prior to joining the Peace Mission Movement. Among those were the Lily-buds, non-virgin women who nevertheless committed to a celibate lifestyle and were therefore "made as virtuous as the Rosebuds" (M. Divine 1982, 32). As is evidenced in their creed, the Lily-buds, too, modeled their lives after the virginity of Mary and the holiness of Jesus, by practicing celibacy and distancing themselves from men:

> To be just like YOUR Spotless Bride; To be pure, clean, undefiled; To always be willing in YOUR Spirit and Mind to abide; To always be sweet, loving and kind; To never hold friendly conversations with the opposite sex—only on business, as YOU have said; To express holiness and virtue, wherever we may be. (Father Divine's International Peace Mission Movement [no date], emphasis original)

We should note, moreover, that virginity and celibacy became increasingly more important in the Peace Mission Movement over time. For instance, Satter (1996, 63) argues that while Divine praised the Rosebuds in the mid-1940s primarily for their "skills" in buying property in areas usually restricted to whites, by 1950, his emphasis had shifted toward an admiration of their virginity. She explains this new emphasis on virginity as linked to Divine's conviction of the millennial role of the United States. Without necessarily denying this statement, an overlap in years could however also lead one to conclude that the emphasis on chastity coincided with his marriage to Mother Divine, in 1946.

In fact, while Divine emphasized in his speeches that Ms. Ritchings was a Rosebud, a virgin, it is important to note that his first wife, Peninnah, was not. However, Divine claims that this first or initial Mother Divine (Peninnah) had expressed a desire for a Rosebud body—a body uncorrupted by sexual desire and intercourse—which points to the importance of chastity in the Peace Mission Movement. It is therefore not a leap to suggest that the increasing importance of celibacy and Divine's spiritual union with Ritchings, also known as Mother Divine, do in fact intersect. For Divine, his marriage to a virgin bride furthered the establishment of the Kingdom of God, and would help to redeem humanity. In other words, Divine's teachings on the necessity of celibacy became much more immediate and urgent after marrying a Rosebud, Ms. Ritchings, in 1946. Now that, in "Year One", the Kingdom of God was ushered in, it was much more imperative that followers would refrain from sexual intercourse, as only abstinence would allow them to be redeemed.

Given that Peninnah was a woman of African American descent, it seems important to emphasize that Mother Divine's identity should therefore be understood across two distinct bodies: first, a black body, and subsequently a white one. Although Peninnah passed away sometime in the early 1940s, Divine did not make this public until he married his second wife, Ritchings, whom he then claimed was Peninnah's reincarnation (Griffith 2001, 143).[9] Reincarnation was, incidentally, a central theme in some New Thought teachings (M. Divine 1982, 51). According to Watts (1992, 23, 168-9), Divine was probably inspired on this score by Charles Fillmore, an important figure in the New Thought movement, who argued that when people became one with God, they would attain a new body, and thereby secure immortality. However, for those who were unable to achieve this goal, reincarnation would offer another chance at attaining eternal life. After his wedding to Ritchings, Divine incorporated a similar take on reincarnation in his own theology: while he encouraged each of his followers to strive for immortality, reincarnation became, in select cases such as that of Peninnah, a welcome alternative. For instance, Divine shared this with his followers in 1946:

> Mother Divine [Peninnah] sought in all sincerity in consciousness while she was with ME, to have a Rosebud's body. She said she desired to go and come in a Rosebud's body! A Rosebud's body as incorruptible and undefiled as could be, was drawn directly to ME through many years of

correspondence and through loving ME and serving ME in all sincerity! [...] Mrs. Divine [Ritchings], as you see Her, is the reproduction and reincarnation of the spirit and the nature and the characteristics of Mother Divine! (F. Divine 1946)

Peninnah, Divine reasoned, had "shed her body" upon realizing that she needed a "new body" to be able to further assist Divine in establishing the Kingdom of God on earth. Divine claimed, furthermore, that Ritchings was a reincarnation and personification of the Virgin Mary, as was Peninnah before her. In other words, the three women are considered to be closely connected: the Virgin Mary was understood to be reincarnated in Peninnah, and, upon her passing, in Ms. Ritchings, who was understood to be a reincarnation of both Mary and Peninnah. Divine's new, reincarnated "Spotless Virgin Bride" [Ritchings] thus served as the so-called "sample and example" of the Virgin Mary. Their marriage—spiritual, interracial, and international—served as a visualization of the Holiness of Jesus Christ and the virginity of Mary, and thus the "perfection of humanity".

To be sure, Divine also taught his creed of "perfection" prior to his wedding to Ritchings. Thus, already in 1938 he would say things like, "the spirit of perfection will be transmitted [through being in the presence of God] and you will become to be the reincarnators [sic] of it. Perfection is developed in the minds of those who will concentrate of the Perfect picture" (F. Divine 1965). However, there is evidence that he regarded his wedding with his second, white, wife as much more important than his first marriage. For instance, he claimed that only with her on his side, the virtue of Mary and Holiness of Jesus could be personified (F. Divine 1976, 21). Elsewhere, Divine states that the "marriage of FATHER and MOTHER Divine Has Given License to the Union of God and Man" (F. Divine 1965). Furthermore, as noted above, Divine's second marriage was so important that the year 1946 became "year one". Inspired by New Thought teachings on visualization, Divine (1974a, 3) reasoned that his marriage demonstrated, in real life, the actualization of the Kingdom of God. In other words, the spiritual union of a black man with a white virgin would usher in the Kingdom of God and redeem humanity. Importantly, though, in the photograph that (re) presents this unity, it is not visualized as a unity of difference, but rather of sameness, as Father and Mother Divine assume a similar color. As such, these photos image and imagine a hybrid body as the future, eternal bodies of the Kingdom of God. Enforcing celibacy was crucial to fulfill the two main goals of the movement, namely the establishment of the Kingdom of

God, and living the reality of heaven on earth; the photographs link this practice to Divine's post-racial imaginaries.

CELIBACY AND NEW BODIES

Celibacy was thus a necessary requirement if one wanted to be saved—and to perhaps live forever. Starting in the 1940s, Divine began to preach that if followers practiced celibacy, they could possibly achieve *physical* immortality. Divine rejected the concept of the afterlife, arguing instead that people should advocate for a heaven on Earth—which, as noted above, from the 1940s on was increasingly more thought to be located in America. In *The Peace Mission Movement* (1982), Ms. Ritchings [Mother Divine] elaborates on this idea when she makes a connection between celibacy, death, and birth. According to her, celibacy is a requirement to achieve eternal life. When humans refrain from propagating, she argues, they will cease to die (M. Divine 1982, 52). The Peace Mission Movement, as stated, does not "do" death. Perhaps we find the best evidence for this claim in the fact that Peninnah's death remained unacknowledged until Divine found, in the body of a white Canadian, her reincarnated spirit.

But refraining from sexual intercourse and other instances of "self-denial" also had more immediate consequences: it would award devoted angels with a new body. Consider, for instance, a section entitled "The Miracle of Good Health" in a 1974 edition of *The New Day*, which reprinted conversations Divine had on health issues. We can read that Divine told one of his disciples, a woman with "eye trouble", that if she adheres to "self-denial", she will be born again without disabilities. He says, "[i]f you have a New Birth of Freedom under GOD, you should be free from all barriers and all limitations and all obstructions, all adverse and undesirable conditions because you become to be a New Creature characteristically, and hence, you are made new physically by the New Birth" (F. Divine 1974b, 11).

Griffith argues convincingly that Divine taught, upon complete conversion, that the bodies of his followers would be created anew. When asked when they were born, followers would list the year that they became a follower of Divine, because that was the year that they were born again (Griffith 2001, 141). It is important to emphasize that we have to understand this transformation in physical terms. Divine would convince his followers that "when you become to be a different one characteristically, dispositionally, naturally and actually as well as mentally and spiritually, you become to be new creatures physically and your bodies will take on new cell tissues in the remodeling and the renovating of your body in which you are now living" (F. Divine 1939, cited in Griffith 2001, 139). All individual parts of the bodies of followers would be completely renewed upon conversion, such as "the blood in your veins", the "heart-beat", and even followers' "odor" (ibid.). Griffith demonstrates that Divine's teachings on the renovation of the body were, again, an adapted version of New Thought ideas—specifically those on health, positive thinking, and the materialization of thought (141).

Griffith makes an important case for the study of materiality and physicality in the Peace Mission movement. However, in concentrating primarily on salvation through various food practices, she has downplayed the role of celibacy in the creation of new, material bodies. Likewise, albeit in an altogether different register, previous scholarship on celibacy in the Peace Mission Movement, primarily that of Kahan (2009) and Satter (1996), has focused exclusively on how Divine's plea for celibacy challenged racial and sexist *discourses*, thereby also overlooking this "physical dimension" of Divine's theology and practice. Kahan seems to subscribe to a discursive understanding of the body, but because his work is not grounded in theory he does not engage in a discussion of the implications of this rather limited viewpoint. Put in stronger terms: his analysis is incomplete, as Kahan seems to suggest that the body, for Divine, is *solely* a symbol—the body as a text, which can be rewritten. Precisely because Kahan does not wrestle with the question of what the body actually is, he does not seem to realize that for Divine, bodies are also physical realities. In *Embodiment and Black Religion*, we are concerned with the "compound body", or the interplay between material and discursive bodies. Divine was not only concerned with refashioning the narratives of discursive (black) bodies, but also with remodeling the physical bodies of his followers. In fact, propagating the very act of living a celibate life involves, we would suggest, a preoccupation with the materiality of the body (see also Olson 2008).

As indicated, Griffith does reflect on material bodies in the Peace Mission Movement, yet while she aptly observes that Divine taught that (physical) bodily perfection was attainable on Earth, she offers no insight as to what these bodies would, according to Divine, *look* like. To be sure, they would have new cells, new veins, new odors, but this tells us little about their physical appearance. However, if we go beyond the means of textual analysis that Griffith employs, and take photographic images seriously as source material, we catch, quite literally, a glimpse of what Divine imagined these new, physical or material bodies to be(come): an off-white, hybrid body. Divine's spiritual wedding—the embodiment of hybridity, a wedding between the Divine and human, a wedding culminating in a grayish, unified complexion—served as a "sample and example" for his followers.

Indeed, we suggest that Divine's teachings on celibacy are imperative if we want to fully understand the force, meaning, and purpose of the artificially discolored bodies. That is, these photos should not be understood, we suggest, as part of one of the many images of the couple, with the sole difference that these just "happen to be" artificially colored. Rather, because they capture, visualize and seemed to have been distributed in honor of their marriage, these images, when understood as performances that aim at creating—if only temporarily—new identities and subjectivities, could be said to offer an idea of what (new) bodies in the Kingdom of God look like. As such, they convey a particular, and significant, performative function in Divine's post-racial imaginary.

HYBRID BODIES IN THE PEACE MISSION MOVEMENT

The artificial coloring of a celibate white and black body in the Peace Mission movement should be understood as the culmination of several "post-racial" performances. To employ the terms "dark complexion" and "light complexion" when referring to skin color and the alternate seating arrangements during Divine's famous banquets are examples of particular racial performances that aimed at the creation of integrated interracial communities, through establishing "race-neutral" discourses that reject white and black racial identities. Here, we abide by a number of scholars that have argued that racial identity is always and already performed (Johnson 2003; Young 2010). Such an understanding of the nature of identity implies that cultural, social, and racialized identities require continuous and constant enactment, also known as performativity, which inscribes identity (and thus such categories as race and gender) onto a body (Butler 1990, 25). Understood in this way, race (or gender, as we will explore in Chapter 4) is thus never a noun, but a process, or as Judith Butler notes in *Gender Trouble*, a "doing", which requires a constant performance.

The repetitive acts of alternate seating arrangements and the conscious deployment of ostensibly race-neutral phrases such as "light complexion" and "dark complexion" are performances that do not only contribute to the inception of a particular community, but also attempt to initiate new identities and subjectivities. Indeed, the performativity of such discourses lies in the fact that they make what they describe, at least within the spatial and temporal parameters of the performance (cf. Nyong'o 2009, 171).[10] For Divine, race-neutral discourses were essentially what Michele Elam (2011, 106) has termed a "performative doing", which implies not only that they required continuing enactments of interracial discourses, but also the conscious dismissal of performances of "blackness" and "whiteness". Moreover, turning to the photographs, the artificial (dis)coloring of the bodies of Mother and Father Divine is understood as a performance through which Divine not only sought to negate blackness and whiteness as markers for identity and subjectivity, but also sought to transcend it, exhaust it, in their representation of a new, hybrid body.

D. Soyini Madison (2014, viii) offers a succinct rendition of performance, which will help to further ground our project. She writes of performance as a form of "cultural staging", thereby emphasizing how performances are "conscious, heightened, reflexive, framed, contained", and operate within a limited temporal frame. We deploy the moniker here to interpret the images of Mother and Father Divine as the conscious staging of post-racial identities. We argue that the making of such a photograph is at once the performance of a particular racialized identity—here, specifically, a hybrid identity—as well as the visual representation of this identity. At stake are not just the static images, but also the particular way in which they were invented and manipulated, and functioned as a performative image that represents the new, post-racial body. These photographs do something: they aim to produce a particular (image) of a body, to produce a particular discourse of what a body should look like—as argued above in our discussions of celibacy—and, despite the fact that many unaltered images of Divine and his wife exist, these particular bodies are significant and have a performative function because they can be argued to (re)present what redeemed bodies in the Kingdom of God could or should look like.

The language of performance, moreover, allows us to negotiate between "reality" and "fiction", "real" and "constructed" (see Taylor 2003). In other words, the fact that these images were clearly staged does not mitigate their representational and performative power and implications. Followers—as well as onlookers—know, even see, that these photos are manipulated, yet they continue to have creative power. Divine's manipulated images thus sought to communicate to his followers a particular message and knowledge: a glimpse of a post-racial, hybrid body as the (future) inhabitant of the Kingdom of God on Earth.

Divine employed the medium of photography to create a particular image that served to transcend racial and fixed notions of blackness, and create a new racial identity. This *hybrid* identity is different from such notions as "interracial" and "race-neutral", which do not necessarily pertain to the creation of a new racial identity, although they do certainly seek to negotiate and even negate the effects and implications of a predetermined blackness and whiteness. The wedding pictures are performances that, to paraphrase Nicole Fleetwood (2011, 6), make the post-racial "visibly knowable". In such performances, the post-racial emerges not simply as "race-neutral" but as *hybrid*. That is, despite his own claims to the contrary, Divine did not ignore race, but, with these images, offered the hybrid body as a new racialized identity. From this, it is possible to conclude, for Divine, that the solution to the problem of the color line, to racism, to discrimination, ultimately lies in the hybrid body.[11]

The performances that are central to this chapter—refusing to use "black" and "white", alternate seating arrangements and, most importantly for our purposes, the artificial (dis)coloring of official portraits and wedding images—can all be understood as expressions of the "quest for complex subjectivity". To be sure, Pinn's theory of religion pertains to the shift from objectified identities towards a posture that holds the multiple "ontological possibilities" in creative tension—not necessarily the transcendence of "blackness" altogether. Still, we suggest that these performances can be understood as the result of Divine's wrestling with predetermined and fixed (racial) categories that objectified his black body. As, for instance, Divine's push for alternate seating arrangements during the banquets suggests, Divine refused to submit to the segregated space that his body was assigned by a racialized and racist American society.[12] Moreover, the artificial coloring of his own black body offered him an opportunity to convey a more complex—if fraught—image and idea of his black body, and black bodies more generally. In "managing" and taking control of his own physical body—that is, the depiction of the physical appearance of his body—as well as that of his wife, Divine actively resisted normative discourses and the symbolic/discursive bodies of black and white followers. Depicting new bodies, Divine placed himself—his own body—as the "sample and example" of future eternal bodies in the post-racial imaginary that was to be the Kingdom of God on Earth.

These images, then, position the body at the center of Divine's post-racial imaginaries. It is through the artificial discoloring of a white and a black body that Divine seeks to convey his post-racial vision for America. This seems to suggest that, to move "beyond" race, beyond the racial identities of whiteness and blackness, requires not only the refusal of racial terminology, but an actual—if solely ocular and thus discursive—change in the form of an artificially altered set of photographs. Furthermore, as stated

28 *Embodiment and Black Religion*

above, these images make the post-racial visibly knowable and provide it with a particular look, a texture, and a feel. Divine opted to present to the world a manipulated image of his black body, an image in which his blackness was negated, transcended, and overcome, thereby also inverting the more common artificial treatment of photographs of African Americans that resulted, purposefully, in a much darker complexion for black subjects.[13] This also suggests that Divine's teachings on the "perfection of humanity" through celibacy and a post-racial America are, albeit implicitly, linked—and find their combined visual representation in an image of a newly-wed, racially hybrid couple. The concept of hybridity, then, also allows us to see that, in the context of the Peace Mission Movement, racial and religious discourses are intertwined.

POST-SCRIPT: ON CELIBACY AND THE POST-RACIAL

In the images, Divine's teachings on celibacy and patriotism "meet", and, in doing so, depict a new racialized identity. What Divine's distorted photographic images attempted to accomplish was to offer a preemptive glimpse of a post-racial America without a "sense or trace or division among [nations and nationalities] characteristically, politically, socially and otherwise" (F. Divine 1951). And, in contrast to many other post-racial imaginaries, Divine's commitment to celibacy, rather than reproduction, was central to this. In *The Amalgamation Waltz* (2009), Tavia Nyong'o conveys that discourses of hybridity and the longing to move "beyond" race, to transcend race, operate within the framework of heterosexuality, marriage, and human reproductive features. That is, Nyong'o demonstrates how the racial hybrid functions as a vehicle to move into a post-racial future only to the extent that this racial hybrid is produced in and through heterosexual reproduction. Jared Sexton argues for a similar connection between interracial or mixed-race discourses and heteronormativity in his *Amalgamation Schemes* (2008), which explores the relationship between anti-blackness and normative sexuality in said discourses.

In such discourses, the (heterosexual) reproductive body is central to matters of hybridity and amalgamation. The bodies in Father Divine's post-racial utopia, however, offer a way of discussing "hybridity" outside of this framework as, given that the off-white body of Father and Mother represents the "perfection of humanity" precisely and only because the couple entered a celibate marriage, celibacy is central to imagining hybrid bodies. "The biracial child", Nyong'o writes, "cannot conceivably do the work of utopia that we repeatedly impose upon her" (2009, 175). In Divine's post-racial utopia, such a burden is not placed on the child, but on the never-to-be "parents". It is their commitment to sexual abstinence that will usher in the racially hybrid Kingdom of God on Earth. Divine's case is, in fact, interesting precisely because his imagined hybrid bodies are not grounded in or produced by biological reproduction between different races, but a spiritual, celibate marriage between humanity and divinity, Mother and Father Divine. Turning to the distorted wedding pictures demonstrates that the Peace Mission Movement conveys, in a seemingly paradoxical way, that the rejection of reproduction produces hybridity.

However, what could theoretically have had progressive or even subversive potential, not in the least in terms of, to use Lee Edelman's oft-used concept, a heteronormative "reproductive futurity", faded in the flawed appeal of an already impoverished and false American dream. Embodying hybridity, Divine increasingly became more committed to mainstream white America, and in the 1950s even lauded the United States as a "racially just" society (Satter 1996, 66). Moreover, Father Divine's plea for celibacy in light of his teachings about American ideals is problematic in yet another way too, as already alluded to above. Indeed, we should not overlook the fact that celibacy in a very real way legitimated the fear of miscegenation. In other words, Divine's new embodied racially and metaphysically hybrid identity is produced in contingency with the larger society's rejection of interracial sexual relationships that could produce mixed-race children and thus "pollute" the ostensible "pure" white race.

NOTES

1. We would like to thank the Peace Mission Movement, in particular Dr. Christopher Stewart, for their cooperation in providing the artificially colored images of Mother and Father Divine that are included in this publication. We should note, moreover, that the Peace Mission movement, after reviewing this chapter, does not agree with our thesis that these artificially colored images create a new racialized identity.
2. We realize that the term "hybrid", in the context of race, is a loaded term as it has often been used to dehumanize and objectify black bodies. Moreover, we are aware of the fact that when discussing embodiment, the term "hybrid" is usually reserved for either mixed-race people, or the merging of technology and flesh. In the case of Divine, there is no biological/physical "mixing" of races, nor a unification of human bodies and technology; rather, we employ the term here as a useful conceptual and analytical framework to denote the creation of post-racial bodies and identities. For other usages of the concept

of "hybrid", see the work of Bhabha (2004) and Young (2001) in post-colonial theory, and Lyotard (1984) in post-modernism.
3 Given that we are primarily interested in the bodies these images portray, and specifically in the fact that these bodies have been artificially (dis)colored, we will not provide a thick description of the images. It is sufficient to note that these were taken during, or on the heels of, the wedding that secured, according to the Peace Mission movement, the union between God and man and as such allowed for the materialization of the Kingdom of God on Earth.
4 We should note that Divine never used the term "post-racial" himself. However, his teachings could be couched as an early post-racial imaginary. The twenty-first century, in particular the years since Barack Obama took office, has witnessed a steady increase in studies that are concerned with post-racial, post-black and/or mixed-race bodies and identities. Given this seemingly sudden upsurge, the idea of the post-racial might seem a contemporary development. However, the post-racial and related issues have a long and complex history. Divine's movement should be understood as part of this history.
5 We should note that the Peace Mission Movement rejects the use of the name George Baker.
6 Satter (1996) has argued that seventy-five to ninety percent of Divine's disciples were black women, although she acknowledges that some of his communes on the West Coast had more Caucasian followers.
7 Likewise, Divine also considered gender a product of the mind, and eschewed gender distinctions. He often referred to himself as both male and female, father and mother, and it is known that at least some of his female followers took on masculine "angelic" names when they joined the movement (Watts 1992: 35; Satter 1996: 55). However, we should note that Divine also ordered his "angels" to segregate according to gender. That is, while black and white were supposed to intermingle, male and female should remain separate. For Divine, sexual segregation—and racial integration—in the Peace Mission movement exemplified living the reality of heaven on earth. This emphasis on sexual segregation seems to radically oppose Divine's statement that gender identification was a product of the mind, which can be abolished. To our best knowledge, Divine never resolved this apparent tension.
8 In arguing for the theological and eschatological necessity of celibacy for Divine, we challenge previous scholarship that has understood the plea for sexual abstinence primarily in light of practical and economic reasons (Kahan 2009; Watts 1992).
9 Similar to Divine, Peninnah's past is shrouded in mystery. She is simply and only known as "Peninnah Divine".
10 It is evident that outside of the safe performative space of Peace Mission communes, the "colorblind" refusal to acknowledge and use racial terminology was often untenable. Thus, we should consider the extent to which the embodiment of race-neutral discourses was virtually impossible for black followers outside of the Peace Mission, who, due to the "hypervisibility" of blackness, are always perceived and recognized as black bodies.

11 In *The Amalgamation Waltz* (2009), Nyong'o offers an extensive critique of the notion that in our supposed post-racial moment, mixed-race or hybrid bodies are the key to the transcendence of race.
12 Divine often stated that the media manipulated his photographs to darken the color of his skin (Primiano 2009: 107).
13 We realize, of course, that Divine's theology and cosmology at the same time also confirmed, underscored and reinforced fixed notions of blackness, in particular as it pertains to his alleged fear of miscegenation, as noted earlier in the chapter.

Chapter Two

Arm, Leg, Leg, Arm, Head, This is God Body: The Body as a Site of Religious Expression in the Five Percenters

> Arm, Leg, Leg, Arm, Head, this is God body [...] I confess, God in the flesh, live among the serpents, turn arenas into churches.
>
> (Jay Z 2013)

In Chapter 1, we highlighted some of the problematic ways in which Father Divine's practice of celibacy intersected with his post-racial imaginary. In this chapter, we turn our focus to another black religious tradition harboring claims of enfleshed divinity, shifting our emphasis toward an account of how this very claim posits an implicit critique of one major strand of the philosophy of religion: natural theology. What are the implications of a tradition that grounds its claim for the very existence of God in the lived experiences of the black body itself? And what would it mean for the philosophy of religion to take such a theology seriously?

The lyrics that opened this chapter come from Jay-Z's song 'Heaven' (2009). Although he makes references to his material successes, the song itself is an extended explanation of *how* he is able to secure such achievements. With careful attention to the song's lyrics, the explanation becomes rather clear: the persona Jay-Z takes on in the song is a deity. But more than that: it is an embodied one, a "god in the flesh", one whose very existence is the reason for his success.

The lyrics of 'Heaven' bear the mark of a less well-known group of people—the Five Percenters, alternatively known as the Nation of Gods and Earths. In fact, many of the lines are expressions of Five Percenter culture. As we will see, "Arm, Leg, Leg, Arm, Head" is more than a rap line; it is an acronym for ALLAH, which, in Five Percenter parlance, speaks to the very existence of God in and through the flesh, through the physical limbs and appendages that make up the black (male) body. This God is not removed, but rather *is* the black man himself. It is for this reason that throughout the song we hear Jay-Z taking on the role of the divine, alluding to—if not outright claiming—a divinity that is not simply present in him, but manifest through his very embodied existence.

It would seem that Jay-Z's lyrics in 'Heaven' clue us into a critical space in religious studies—the philosophy of religion. What we see in Jay-Z's lyrics, but more importantly in the Five Percenter way of life, is an approach to an understanding of the black body (particularly the black male body) that stands as the development of a more expansive philosophy of religion—or, more specifically, natural theology—aimed at speaking to the dynamism and complexity of black people, and black men more specifically. In other words, the Five Percenters develop an ontological proof for God's existence in and through their embodied existence as black men and women. This ontological proof is made possible not by appeals to *a priori* reasoning, but rather in and through the black body itself; and, by tethering God's existence to the existence of the black (male) body, Five Percenters instill dignity and worth in themselves, providing a greater sense of self in relation to their communities and the world. In short, the Five Percenters develop, and indeed live, an embodied natural theology that speaks to a push for greater life meaning. We will first examine this push within the movement's history, before moving into a discussion of some of its salient philosophical contributions.

FIVE PERCENTERS IN HISTORICAL CONTEXT

The Five Percenters emerged in 1960s New York City as an alternative to the rigid theology and ritual practices of the Nation of Islam (NOI). After having been reprimanded by the NOI in 1964, Clarence 13X, a former trainee in the "Advanced Fruit of Islam" (AFOI), separated from the NOI. Many reasons are given for this separation, some of which concern Clarence 13X's violation of the NOI codes of conduct due to his gambling habits and drug use, but one thing is certain: during his involvement with the NOI, Clarence 13X reconstructed some of the movement's core doctrines—doctrines that would have incredible appeal among many of the city's young black men.

One of the most important doctrinal shifts concerned the nature of God. Instead of affirming that Allah was only fully incarnate in the man of W. Fard Muhammad, Clarence 13X claimed that *each* Black man, in the very nature of his being, is a God in his own right (as we will discuss later on, in this worldview, women are typically called "Earths" rather than "Gods"). He supported this claim with the NOI's "student enrollment lessons", wherein the identity of the black man is taught: "1. Who is the Original Man? The Original Man is the Asiatic Black Man, the Maker, the Owner, the Cream of the Planet Earth, the Father of Civilization, and God of the Universe" (Nuruddin 1994, 116). Clarence 13X took this statement literally; laying claim to his status as a God, he began to call himself "Allah".[1] Allah suggested that black men's lives could only improve once they realized who and what they already were: "God[s] of the Universe". He called this realization of one's own divinity "coming into knowledge of self", and began to eagerly share this knowledge with others.

But Allah also knew that many people would reject these teachings of knowledge of self. Despite his separation from the NOI, he nevertheless found many of its teachings to be useful. For instance, using the NOI's "Lost-Found Muslim Lesson No. 2", Allah taught his young followers that a person is a member of one of three different groups: the "ignorant 85 percent", the masses of people who are deceived because they believe in a "mystery God" (that is, a transcendent and supernatural divine entity) and do not have knowledge of self; the 10 percent, the small elite who do have knowledge, yet use this knowledge to deceive the 85 percent; and the remaining 5 percent, the "poor righteous teachers", who have knowledge of themselves and are thus supposed to dedicate their lives to sharing this with others (Allah 2009, 121–2; Nuruddin 1994, 116–17). The name "Five Percenters" refers to this teaching, and to the group's self-identification as the righteous teachers who are continuing to relay knowledge of self to others.

With these two shifts in place, other teachings started to develop. Of particular importance to us is the centrality of the body in Allah's teachings. As we have already indicated, these teachings emerged from his persistent claim that, as Gods, black men had complete autonomy over their lives. Fond of clever acronyms, Allah expressed this teaching by turning the very word "Islam" into an acronym for "I, Self, Lord, And Master". For the Five Percenters, Islam thus points to the identity and capabilities of black men instead of naming a religious institution framed by submission to a metaphysical entity. He likewise turned the name of "Allah" into the acronym "Arm-Leg-Leg-Arm-Head",[2] not only describing a God's body but also emphasizing a fundamental link between the black (male) body and its divinity. Taking these two teachings in tandem, the result is a symbolic depiction of the black (male) body as the quintessential expression of individualized freedom. That is to say, for Allah, the body was central to the explication of black (male) freedom, dignity and mobility in the world.

The centrality of the body extends beyond the bodies of black males in the Five Percent Nation. Although women appear relatively late in the development of the movement—they were not present in any formal way until after Allah's release from the Matteawan mental institution in 1967—they were nevertheless incorporated into the Five Percent cosmology in deeply embodied (albeit still problematically patriarchal) ways. As Michael Muhammad Knight aptly explains, the reason for this largely had to do with the stance toward women that Allah seems to have inherited from other patriarchal traditions: "Allah's own concepts of gender roles grew simultaneously from Nation of Islam teachings and the natural patriarchy of life on hard streets where physical might made right and [...] prostitution [was] a mere footnote to survival" (Knight 2007, 209).[3] In the early days, female presence consisted of the "significant others" of the young Gods, who shared with these women Allah's teachings. As the movement grew Allah began to acknowledge the presence of women, calling them "Earths", the bodily and epistemological "soil" within which the Gods plant their bodily and epistemological "seeds". Often understood in a twofold fashion, the term "seed" refers to both the man's semen as well as his understanding of the teachings (Allah 2009, 125). This framing rendered the black female body a physical and intellectual reservoir for the male's various deposits.

If the black male body is understood as the vessel of unmitigated freedom and mobility, the bodies of the earths are framed in terms of submission. Given female reproductive abilities, the Earths are given domestic roles, often finding themselves taking care of children and making sure the home is maintained. Musicologist Felicia Miyakawa (2005, 34) explains: "While Gods are free to choose their own paths in life, the role of Earths is somewhat more restricted [...] The main goal for an Earth is reproduction because through reproduction a woman symbolizes the life-giving forces of the earth." Earths occupy a role that has been often understood as "secondary but absolutely necessary", and this has raised questions concerning the treatment by the NGE (Nation of Gods and Earths, another name for the Five Percenters) of its female members. While Miyakawa (2005, 48) raises questions concerning patriarchy and oppression of women within the movement, she ultimately concludes that the women do not typically "consider themselves oppressed or restricted. Instead, they embrace their roles with joy [...] Most importantly, these women feel beloved [sic], protected, and respected". While it may very well be the case that the designation of Earth is aimed at instilling dignity and value in black women through their bodies, from our vantage point the roles assigned to Earths do not seem to afford them the same degree of mobility and freedom. For example, Gods frequently partner with multiple Earths without issue, while Earths are usually encouraged to remain monogamous with one God (Knight 2007, 208). Such inequity stems from particular ontological claims regarding the men and women, and continues to raise questions concerning the position of women in the movement. While responding to these issues in more detail is beyond the scope of this chapter, it is important to note that some women have also started to take the moniker "God" as their title, eschewing "Earth" and all of the patriarchal and possibly misogynistic implications that this title entails (Knight 2011, Kindle location 247).

Although it is clear that Allah understood the acronym **A**rm, **L**eg, **L**eg, **A**rm, **H**ead to be specifically correlated with the black *male* body, it would seem that its generality makes it possible for women to occupy this role as well. That is, the fact that most bodies, male and female alike, are equipped with two arms, two legs, and a head seems to leave open the theoretical possibility of women occupying this role. Hence, we will remain sensitive to this formulation by referring to Gods more inclusively as black *wo/men*.

WHO IS GOD? GOD IN FIVE PERCENTER THOUGHT AND LIFE

We have already alluded to the centrality of the body in Five Percenter life and culture in terms of both its symbolic and physical significance. But more than this, the body also serves as the existential and philosophical justification *for* their identities as Gods and Earths. Put differently, black bodies operate as the twofold proof (cosmological and ontological) for God's existence. To be clear, the Five Percenters do not understand their mode of existence as explicitly religious. For them, "religion" entails a belief in the traditional God of the three monotheistic religions—a God whose existence the Five Percenters vehemently deny. For them, God does not exist on some supernatural plane, hovering above all of existence as the result of God's ingenuity. Instead, we find them exploring godhood in terms of embodiment and the everyday movements of bodies. While our purpose here is not to make claims for or against the existence of God, we do understand "God" to be used as a discursive construct that can, particularly in the case of the Five Percenters, provide a greater sense of self in relation to one's community and the world more generally.

In traditional philosophy of religion, cosmological proofs are understood in terms of *causality*. Consider, for instance, Thomas Aquinas's argument for efficient causes. From his perspective, simply tracing each effect back to its cause can prove God's existence; by looking at what caused what, we find ourselves ultimately asking what caused the universe. Aquinas will argue that the ultimate cause of the universe is the "unmoved mover", the entity that puts all of existence in motion. God, then, is that which causes everything else—or at least is that which starts and perpetuates the causal chain, engendering and maintaining the existence of the cosmos.

We find an almost near perfect correlate in Five Percenter thought and life. From the Five Percenter perspective, the black wo/man is God precisely by virtue of her or his being *black*. At a natural-historical level, the Five Percenters trace their existence as black people back to Africa, which they claim is the source of all earthly existence. This claim is substantiated by geographical, geological, and genetic history (a theme we treat in more detail in Chapter 9). As is becoming increasingly known, the continent that is now labeled Africa was the place where the first human beings emerged—hence, the first people were *African*. By connecting their genealogy to Africa, the Five Percenters make a natural-historical claim to being the original people. Knight puts it this way: "The original members of the human race, the first to conceptualize things like 'God' and 'ethical responsibility', were black [...] humans [who] migrated out of eastern Africa, and would eventually cover the globe" (Knight 2011, Kindle location 247).

But this natural-historical claim merely serves as context; there is a genealogical claim here that cannot be understated. Because of black people's skin color, the Five Percenters make a genealogical connection to the original people, arguing that the essence of this originality exists in their very bodies. Five Percenters then extend this connection to original humanity in order to argue that the black body also bears the mark of divinity, the very essence of godhood. It is here where the acronym ("Arm, Leg, Leg, Arm, Head") for Allah, or God in Arabic, gains its full force and significance. The black body—and precisely as *black*—is the very embodiment of Allah, comprising a divine system of physical appendages and parts that cannot be denied once one comes into proper knowledge of self. "Arm, Leg, Leg, Arm, Head", then, is the linguistic expression of the divinity that is the black body; it is a "God body", "God in the flesh", the physical proof that God does indeed exist in the form of a black embodied human *being*.

Such an understanding of God certainly has some important implications for natural theology. Philosopher Brian Davies (2000, 175) defines natural theology as "a philosophical enterprise which advances conclusions about divinity based on purely rational reflection". That is, natural theology does not rely on doctrinal framings to substantiate its proofs for or against God's existence. If this is the case, then this claim to godhood from within the purview of natural history becomes a cosmological proof *par excellence*. Indeed, if one follows the history of natural theology, one finds that its central aim was to provide a proof for God's existence without appealing to doctrinal texts or traditional framings. Philosophically, the argument might look something like this:

(1) Africans were the original people.
(2) As original people, Africans were the progenitors of all human life, making them the ultimate cause of human life and existence.
(3) Because black people bear the mark of "Africanness" in their phenotypical traits—that is, in their skin tone and physiology—they stake a claim as being the most direct descendants of the original African people.
(4) As direct descendants of the original people, black people bear in their bodies the mark of divinity itself.
(5) Because the black body bears the mark of divinity, the black body itself is *proof* of God's existence—not in some supernatural realm, but rather in the here and now. Gods live among us in the form of black wo/men.

The arguments above are logically consistent and thereby render this particular natural-historical approach to black embodiment a coherent proof of God's existence.

This cosmological proof via natural history is coupled with another, ontological proof, grounded in the existential-phenomenological reality the Five Percenters face—which is to say, the lived experience of being black. To be sure, the ontological proof provided by the Five Percenters differs substantially from those handed down through the western philosophical tradition. In the West, the ontological proof has its origins in Anselm of Canterbury and has been developed over time by other thinkers such as René Descartes. In essence, the ontological proof claims that God's existence can be substantiated via logical (not empirical or experiential) evidence. St. Anselm (2000, 311–12), for example, framed it this way: God is the being for whom no greater being could be conceived. In other words, the human capacity to imagine a supreme being invokes God's existence at an *a priori* level. Descartes' ontological argument claims that existence is a perfection, and because God is necessarily the author of perfection, then God must exist. God exists because *existence* exists (Descartes 2000,

327–9). While the cosmological argument brings God into the purview of the ultimate cause of existence itself, the ontological argument demonstrates God's existence as a necessary precondition of existence itself.

Immanuel Kant (cited in Davies 2000, 337–41) and Martin Heidegger (Heidegger 2002, 42–74) have each in their own way attempted to deconstruct the ontological argument on logical and phenomenological grounds. Kant argues that "existence is not a predicate", which means that existence is not a *feature* of the world, but rather is the very condition for the world itself and therefore doesn't require God. Heidegger takes another route, deconstructing western natural theology as necessarily onto-theological—that is, the God of the universe only serves as ground and foundation for being without articulating what the meaning of being *is* (Heidegger 2002, 42–74). In so doing, both Kant and Heidegger alert us to the fact that ontological arguments, at least as presented by Descartes, Anselm, and others, are unfeasible.

The Five Percenters provide an ontological proof for God's existence that avoids the sorts of logical abstractions that plagued Descartes and Anselm, as they unequivocally employ a different kind of ontological argument—one that emerges not from the sphere of reason and formal logic, but rather out of the context of their lived experiences. It is here where a phenomenological analysis of the Five Percenters' approach is helpful, that is, a thick description of the conditions, structures, and contexts that shape the contours of lived experience.

The Five Percenters originate out of two inextricably connected contexts: the racially charged 1960s and the religious milieu of the Nation of Islam. Like the NOI, the Five Percenters' theological claims are as much about race as they are about God; they have as much to do with the concrete existential realities of African Americans as with understanding the ultimate cause of the universe. This point cannot be overstated: when understood as an existential-ontological response to the racial and socio-political context out of which the Five Percenters emerged, their teachings speak to an affirmation of black *being*, an expression of the value and worth of black existence.

Being is important here. The racially tense context from which the Five Percenters emerged created a rich space in which the claims of Clarence 13X could flourish in the life-worlds of young black men struggling with a system that denied them recognition and opportunity. Lewis Gordon (1994) and Frantz Fanon (1967) speak of this denial of recognition and opportunity in philosophical terms: Gordon relates this to existential invisibility, and Fanon discusses this denial and lack of recognition as the relegation of black people to a zone of non-being. Both thinkers convey that the anti-black world of the 1960s produced a phenomenological context wherein the black body operated as negative matter, the negative space within which whiteness and white people flourished. Trapped in this zone of non-being, the Five Percenters developed a language and praxis that were responsive to this existential-phenomenological context; only they reframed their very existence as an expression of the divine. If blacks were deemed "negative matter", if blacks had their very visibility attached to their objectification, then the knowledge of self as God (or, for that matter, as Earth) constitutes an ontological reversal. "Knowledge of self" became reclamation of black being from the zone of non-being, from the negation of black existence as having inestimable value and worth. In reframing and repurposing their very bodies, they arrived at an ontological proof. For the Five Percenter, the body, which we understand in this book as a "compound body", thus serves as the locus for the quest for complex subjectivity.

With regard to framings, consider the freedom we spoke of earlier with regard to the acronyms ALLAH and ISLAM. Arm, Leg, Leg, Arm, Head, when in combination with I, Self, Lord, And Master, become the expression of bodily freedom, an affirmation of black life through the body's mobility. Allah's acronymic affirmations spoke of the godhood of black men through the freedom of their bodies. While the NOI often restricted black people by offering salvation through strict bodily and religious guidelines—that is, by claiming that one still needed to submit to W. Fard Muhammad and dress a particular way—Allah argued that Gods had freedom to operate however they chose. For Allah, each man is a God, he is able to live his life however he pleases; there is no agreed-upon ethical code or established set of norms to which each God should submit. A God's way of living is thus completely up to him, producing considerable fluidity and flexibility within the Five Percent Nation. Knight recalled an experience where he heard one God denounce marijuana, only to be followed up by another God who endorsed its use (2007, 23). The very existence of the body—that is, its existential function as a vessel of mobility and perception—is one way Allah clued his followers into their ontological godhood.

Allah did this in other ways as well—particularly as it related to the process of "show and prove", or speaking one's truth, applying the teachings in conversation and community with others. One's existence as a God is demonstrated through the ability to build upon, "science out", recite and use the lesson in a way that shows and proves one's godhood. The black body lives this ontological proof—not by way of abstract logical reasoning, but rather through the cultivation, development, and maintenance of the divine lessons passed on from God to God, from Five Percenter to Five Percenter.

But there is more than the freedom of the body and showing and proving that constitutes the embodied ontological proof of the Five Percenters. The early Five Percenters were taught self-defense and to value a healthy lifestyle and the capacity to procreate (Allah 2009, 13). Allah followed Elijah Muhammad's dietary laws, which included fasting and a healthy diet (as we will explore briefly in Chapter 8), and urged the early Gods to do the same. In fact, part of the training to achieve knowledge of self is a three-day fast (Allah 2009, 133). Allah taught that, through fasting it was possible to absorb the lessons more quickly and to speed up the process of self-discovery. In these three areas—the body's freedom, showing and proving, and the cultivation of a strong and healthy body (in particular for procreation)—the Five Percenters live their divine existence; in their very being, in and through their "compound body", they are the proof of their own divinity.

In light of this, the kind of rational deconstructions of the ontological proof provided by philosophers become irrelevant. For the Five Percenters, existence is not a predicate of being. They do not see their existence as a characteristic of who they are, but rather understand their very existence as divine. Moreover, Heidegger's onto-theological critique—the critique that there is one ground for all of existence, and that this very ground does not answer the question of the meaning of existence—is answered through their embodied movement and freedom as well. There is no *one* ontological ground for existence, as each and every God grounds his (and, increasingly, her) individual existence, while the community of Gods and Earths speaks to a collective ground for Five Percenter existence. No singularity means there is no *causa sui*, no singular transcendent philosophical or theological ground from within which all Gods move. The meaning of existence is constantly changing and expanding, as it is worked and re-worked in the thought and practice of Five Percenter daily life. Both the cosmological and ontological proofs provided by the Five Percenters operate as attempts to speak to a more expansive understanding of black *being*, one that highlights the complexity of black life without reducing it to non-being or negative matter.

CONCLUDING THOUGHTS

Now that we have established a connection between the philosophy of religion and the Five Percenters' thought and life, it is important to return to the overarching claim guiding this chapter: the Five Percenter way of life provides a critique of the philosophy of religion. And in so doing, their way of life attunes us to the possibility of a more expansive understanding of religion—one that extends far beyond the limitations of a traditionally theistic theological approach.

Consider this: in both the cosmological and ontological proofs demonstrated by the Five Percenters, the body remains central. The centrality of the body cannot be overstated. Given the fact that traditional philosophy of religion usually is an enterprise framed by questions of religious experience, the existence and apprehension of God, the problem of evil, the problem of miracles, and so on, the Five Percenters can be seen as providing a critical disruption of this framework. Close attention to their way of life provides new methodological inroads for the philosophy of religion by attuning the philosophical approach to religion to the complexities and vicissitudes of daily life.

This bodily approach deconstructs the rigidity and sterility marking rationalist approaches to the philosophy of religion. Indeed, if the philosophical study of religion is to take seriously the breadth and depth of religious life, thought, and experience, it must *necessarily* engage the tone and tenure of the infinitely complex world of lived human experience. Otherwise, it becomes a failed enterprise with a data set that is too limited and too antiquated to take seriously the contemporary and historical contexts within which we find ourselves as human beings.

But this bodily approach does more than provide new philosophical inroads as it also invites reflection on religion in more expansive terms. More specifically, by centering the body, the Five Percenters engage in the quest for complex subjectivity. We can gather as much from the way they trace their lineage back to Africa in the cosmological proof, and see it even stronger in the way they speak to the body's freedom, live out their existence as Gods and Earths, and embrace the centrality of the body through the voluntary adoption of certain physical practices. By "showing and proving", fasting, and "sciencing out" the nature of the universe, the Five Percenters hold the body central to the process of gaining a more expansive sense of self.

NOTES

1 Clarence 13X will be referred to as Allah for the remainder of the chapter.
2 We borrow this stylized way of typing these terms from Miyakawa (2005: 32).
3 Five Percenters are notoriously secretive—which is what largely accounts for their relative obscurity. With this in mind, we often rely on secondary sources—texts written by people who have either studied closely or have been initiated into the culture—as our source material. Knight, along with other scholars whose work we use in this chapter, such as Felicia Miyakawa, Wakeel Allah and Yusuf Nuruddin, have spent considerable time with the Five Percenters, and we therefore find their work particularly helpful here.

Part Two
Cultural Production

Chapter Three

Making Bodies with a Brush Stroke: African American Visual Art and the Re/constitution of Black Embodiment

The chapters in the previous section raised methodological and theoretical concerns, but also questions about where and when we might find religion and bodies colliding: the first chapter "found" the body *and* religion in images, the second chapter in rap lyrics and "ciphers". This second section picks up where we left off, demonstrating how the "and" operates in black cultural production. Indeed, if the body is, as we argue here, a principal locus for the quest for complex subjectivity, then this warrants a broader examination of black religion beyond traditional and institutional forms of religious practice. Here, we take up depictions, representations and engagements with the body in African American cultural production, including visual art, literature, film, and certain practices within Black Greek Letter Organizations. This chapter suggests that cultural production is a site in which fuller, more complicated depictions of the body and black life emerge—and by paying attention to this, we hope to offer a more expansive account of black religion.

We begin this work here, with a consideration of the art of Jean-Michel Basquiat. The visual arts, in this case the work of Basquiat, constitute something of a statement of meaning, a mark toward complex subjectivity, over against a social consensus on the lack of value constituted by embodied black bodies. More specifically, this chapter is concerned with an interrogation of the relationship between appropriation and political intent, in particular as it relates to race in Basquiat's paintings 'Grillo' (1984) and 'Flexible' (1984). According to Arthur Danto, art of the late twentieth century has a political dimension, an intentionality that extends beyond the art itself. That is to say, there is a purpose or function to a work of art that pushes beyond questions of aesthetics and instead wrestles with questions related to the socio-political and cultural dimensions of human life. It isn't always clear whether he perceives this as being a useful or harmful situation; this uncertainty is mirrored in a more general debate regarding the relationship between art and politics. However, it is this situation of uncertainty that makes the topic of interest and worth investigation. The discussion of art in this chapter reflects on Danto's argument regarding the politics of art. "In my own view", he writes, "the major artistic contribution of the decade [1970s] was the emergence of the appropriated image—the taking over of images with established meaning and identity and giving them a fresh meaning and identity" (Danto 1997, 15). Yet, do these two—appropriation and political intent—always line up? This question frames the rest of this chapter.

BODIES/ART AND THE ART OF BODIES

The intentionality of the artist at work and the manner in which this intent is shaped by socio-cultural forces for political ends is significant and it informs the artwork's push beyond aesthetics to politics. This importance entails not traditional reflection on aesthetic meaning and location (i.e., the framing of a work's beauty and rightful placement as "art") in the art world per se, but rather assessment of art's significance related to political ends. In this chapter, we are specifically concerned with the political meanings and implications of troubled/troubling depictions of certain bodies. As already noted, we understand the body here as "compound", that is, we are concerned with both the discursive or linguistic construction of the body and its material form. This also affects how we understand art. As Hans Belting notes, "it is through the vast array of images to which humanity accords meaning that the human being proves himself a cultural being, a being that cannot be described solely in biological terms" (Belting 2011, 37). Think in terms of a question: What can be constituted by art, not what can constitute art? The artist reframes the discursive body, and by so doing forces a rethinking and repositioning of the material body. As we already noted in the introduction, there are links between the two modalities of the body: in a sense, we are walking worlds full of images, ideas, and ideals. By manipulating "things" and his/her body as a "tool" of production, the artist is able to foster ways of thinking about, understanding, and addressing bodies and the cultural worlds in which these bodies move.

After all, as Hans Belting remarks, images hold "symbolic meaning and they function to colonize our bodies (our brains)" (Belting 2011, 10). In other words, Belting notes, "images both affect and reflect the changing course of human history" (p. 10). For instance, the image of the "American flag" tends to trigger certain embodied responses and modes of thinking about nation and relationship to nation. The image isn't the body, but rather pushes us to understand and see more into the "form" of different bodies. This process is carried out by the medium—the "something" (e.g., canvas) upon which the image rests. Things are experienced through the body, and "even the virtual body, an extended self perception, happens with the sensory organs of our bodies" (p. 11). Images of all kinds and bodies of all sorts are linked together, intimately related and mutually affecting each other. While this isn't Belting's concern, we would note it is the relationship between the two (image and body) that accounts for the type of socio-political, psychological, and cultural work that art is equipped to do.

Belting argues the body can produce images/pictures and it can also become a picture through modification and decoration (Belting 2011, 22). However, the sketching of race, gender, sexuality, and so on, unto discursive bodies speaks to the production of a certain type of picture meant to depict and support the status quo. Yet, artists have also challenged this by using images, using pictures, and their own bodies to assert a different narrative that subverts dehumanizing and subjugating ways of thinking and doing.

In a sense, this posturing of art/artists amplifies the shift in sensibilities and pushes it forward as a way of presenting dynamics of reified bodies that are not resolved through the civil rights struggles (Danto 1997, 126). Artists became political commentators and activists. Some of what is significant about this positioning has to do with the lessons of plasticity entailed through the awareness of embodiment—its nature and meaning. There is something about art as political act that, as Danto claims in his reflection on pop art, made it "at least a possibility that art, too, might be enlisted in the direct service of humanity" (Danto 1997, 130).

In presenting the body as the content as well as the form of artistic expression, it might just be the case that the artist signifies by: (1) suggesting the falsity of stereotypical presentations and understandings of despised embodied bodies; (2) re-arranging the status quo affirmed occupation of time and space allotted those despised bodies; and, (3) offering an aesthetically arranged alternate metaphysics of embodied bodies. In addition, one might say, as Elizabeth Grosz notes with regard to a Darwinian take on art, that the artist's effort despite any outcomes of the work speaks to the humanity of the despised vis-à-vis the project of the artist in that humanity is reflected in "our ability to represent, to signify, to imagine, to wish for and make ideals, goals, aims" (Grosz 2011, 169).

The body is always entangled with the world, with the stuff of the world, with the things of the world, and with other bodies layered in the world. Art, in this instance, seeks to present these entanglements for observation, for exploration, and for correction. Art manipulates, presents, and represents bodies—and in this way offers a critique of socio-political structures that warp the meaning of bodies and the bodies of meaning. Through art the layered nature of history is presented: the artist has history; the "things" used to construct art have histories; the bodies the artist seeks to signify and trouble have histories; and the body as the artist wants it to be understood has history. Art demonstrates that history is never singular. "What do you see in art?" is a question that captures something of how bodies move through time and space and what this movement means. The question, by extension, is a questioning of circumstances, of "others" and "things" as well as the viewer.

At times, as numerous art historians and critics highlight, artists have done this reconstruction of meaning through a signifying of stereotypical visuals. The embodied African American body remains, for instance, a *black* body. It is safe to say that such artistic attention to blackness does not end the challenges that inhibit the possibility of fully recognizing the value of black bodies, but at the very least art disrupts the standard narrative's visual justification and causes dissonance. Disruption and dissonance constitute a cartography in that art, like mappings, says as much by absence as presence—both outline something but fail to capture everything. Hence, art can be deceptive and manipulative. And, as we shall see, it is this deception—this signification—employed by African American artists that constitutes a compelling component of art's political dimension. Art pokes the membranes of the cultural worlds in which we live. What we have, then, is a visual representation of the manner in which the body is always qualified, never generic (Weiss 1999, 1). Yet, there is a way in which challenging truncated notions of the meaning of the compound body happens through reifying or highlighting particular dimensions of what it means to be embodied. In order to make this point, we turn our attention to the work of Basquiat.

BASQUIAT'S INSIDE/OUT FIGURES

"I wanted to be a star, not a gallery mascot" (Hoban 1998, 116). *Star. Not Gallery mascot.* With this statement, Basquiat asserts his relationship to the art world—to those who sold and collected his art. It is a statement about aesthetics and about bodies to the extent this relationship is framed by assumptions concerning the beauty of both his work and his body.

Basquiat trained himself as a child to think artistically in relationship to the structure and mechanics of the human body vis-à-vis *Gray's Anatomy*. His mother gave him the book when he was hospitalized. And in a certain way, as his broken body recovered, he fed his imagination through images in the textbook of bodies pulled apart. Basquiat encountered his body and, through his drawings, other bodies—all of which are open to manipulation and re/construction in a variety of ways and within multiple overlapping contexts. The hospital workers "held" and inspected his body, while he "handled" and re-presented the bodies in the textbook through art. He experienced his body by viewing and manipulating his body, but in other ways he experienced his body through his "study" of the mapping of other bodies. That is to say, Basquiat's work is both auto/biography in that it presents the cultural history of African Americans as it presents his personal wrestling with the racial trauma of life. In a word, there is something about this early experience of the body as open to "work" that informs Basquiat as a recognized artist.

Coming of artistic age during a period well after abstract expressionism, marked by the remains of pop art, and swaying to the rhythm of hip hop, his work reveals the raw substance of urban life. In some cases it exposes the organs of the compound body so as to make apparent the circumstances defining a given historical moment. As a graffiti "tagger" writing his "name" (SAMO) across New York City, Basquiat was quite familiar with exposé—altering the familiar (the walls of New York City) with new markings that demanded attention and unpacking. In like manner, the exposed organs of some of his figures disrupt the familiar and encourage investigation and exploration of the socio-political implications of bodily difference.

In a way, his images—the compound body exposed—signify the effort to render everything familiar. "Basquiat", writes Marc Mayer, "speaks articulately while dodging the full impact of clarity like a matador. We can read his pictures without strenuous effort—the words, the images, the colors and the construction—but we cannot quite fathom the point that they belabor" (Mayer 2005, 50). Basquiat tells stories that might, at first glance, appear simple; yet, they are more than an arrangement of stick figures. Safeguarding stereotypical depiction is difficult with the inverted bodies (e.g., bodies with organs exposed). Basquiat deconstructs and re-develops bodies in a way that makes reconstituting a comfortable sense of the past difficult at best. He turns blackness into awareness or lucidity of an aesthetic and epistemological sort. He controls the presentation of the image, and determines how much of the inner self is offered for view: What of exposed organs?[1] What of bodies dissected, pulled apart, and displayed? What of words written and denied? Of images fixed, yet floating? What do these "things" speak?

The ostensibly simple depiction of figures such as Jack Johnson offers racial and cultural history. It is a simple image, a black outline with one arm raised, and a crown above the head—with the name just below the torso. It is part of a series of paintings related to black boxers who transformed the sport through their dominance. The viewer has no choice but to look at Johnson; there are no other images, nothing present beyond the crown and his name. In a cultural world that is much more interested in the invisibility of black body, Basquiat highlights them. Through this image, Basquiat imposes the stature of Johnson, demanding the viewer recognize his singularity, through the presentation of his body without ornamentation and distraction. Basquiat provides not only description of black life, but commentary—often present through simple language, lone words printed. He isolates scenarios and personalities and interrogates them for what they can tell us about the current moment.

BODIES EXPOSED: GENERAL THOUGHTS

Projected onto canvas or wood, the inside/out embodied figure, or what we earlier referenced as inverted bodies, promotes a sense of agency and ability that serves to humanize as it serves to confine. Such work raises the question of what it means to be embodied and the degree to which embodiment exposes our more delicate components (e.g., literal and figurative organs). By exposing inner "bits"—or organs—Basquiat allows for multiple perspectives on the body. The rugged application of paint, for instance, speaks visually to the inability to fully render this body docile, to control it completely—although it is viewed somewhat fully. The fluidity of depiction and the blurred lines that mark out the body over against other elements of painting speak to identity in flux—the nature and meaning of the embodied human as vibrant and shifting away from and between perceived boundaries. The medium that accommodated an image actually could be any surface; Basquiat did not limit himself to one particular medium, as he recognized that art—like daily experience—takes place where it takes place and covers those "surfaces" with meaningful messages.[2]

The various surfaces upon which he painted—canvas, wood, mechanical devices, and so on—point to the manner in which bodies are always connected to and represented in/by these cultural worlds. That is to say, his use of medium speaks to the human body's connection to nature (e.g., wood) and social worlds (e.g., mechanical devices). In brief, cultural worlds are already and always impinging upon and impinged upon by bodies. Such materials speak to the world in which bodies are built and to which they refer. Basquiat's inverted bodies, as we will explore in the next section, show some of this vibrant vacancy, but they also show more than this. They speak to the construction of bodies as well as the manner in which this construction can never speak all there is to know about bodies. "Basquiat", writes Dieter Buchhart, "unremittingly pursued the principle of sampling his immediate surroundings, extracting the material that allowed him to step beyond pure painting and load his works with content and references" (Buchhart 2010, xiv). Furthermore, Basquiat's material body, compromised over time by the demands, pleasures, and obsessions of life (e.g., drug use), mirrors the bodies depicted.

BODIES EXPOSED/EXAMINED: TWO EXAMPLES

To clarify our point, we will discuss two pieces, dating back to 1984, said to represent his interest in the socio-cultural circumstances of people of African descent, as evidenced in his style of presentation (Marshall 1993, 15). With 'Flexible' (1984), the exposed body is painted onto a large frame, which was produced by nailing several individual boards together. In this way, it immediately speaks to the intimate connection of the human body to its surroundings.[3] Facing the painting, the left arm of the body reaches up, while the right arm bends down forming something of a "u" shape before reaching up and joining the left. There are no hands discernible, just a portion of the right arm painted green over the black, with white lines marking both arms. The lungs are exposed as they are outlined in white, the left lung larger than the other and what appears to be the stomach is outlined as a red oval. The mouth is open, red, with two rows of white teeth depicting something that could be considered an aggressive expression. The nose is broad and the eyes are open, but don't have pupils; both are outlined in yellow. This face doesn't look like the skulls that Basquiat usually painted, but rather resembles more closely the look of an African mask, a tribal mask attached to a tribal torso. A red line forms a wide circle around the head, crossing the torso of the figure midway. All this is set against a white background—which gives the impression of a black body exposed against a backdrop of whiteness as normative. The body is presented, shaped, and understood over against the background. Although flat and projected against this background of whiteness, the black body speaks to plasticity—or flexibility, in Basquiat's words—that marks out its vitality and supple nature over against the inflexible background. Basquiat presents the image in such a way that it does not render the black body as primitive, lacking connection to culture.

'Grillo' (1984) shows constructed bodies similar to African masks, but these bodies float in the foreground, with signs, symbols, and language around them.[4] A staple of Basquiat's creative palate, these marks, words, and symbols are important. "For drawing", writes Dieter Buchhart, "is the foundation of Basquiat's artistic practice: drawn letters, words, lists and phrases are often an integral component of his work" (Buchhart 2015, 27). Hip hop culture, with which he was deeply familiar, had made the importance of language made visual as a marker of meaning—of ontological and epistemological significance within tough terrains of despair—evident for Basquiat. The words in the painting are tied to bodies that are exposed. In hip hop, bodies dance, they pose, and they present themselves. In Basquiat's art, bodies push against traditional notions of aesthetic value, of placement, and comportment. In an odd way, they resist. Resistance should be understood here along the lines of Sisyphus and his rock, as Albert Camus (1991, 119–23) presents the scenario—a victory, but only on an epistemological level in the form of greater lucidity and awareness. This involves not being what others want you to be, and continuing to move through the world despite angst and trauma. The letters—words and symbols—capture meanings that are related to the body. In this way, flesh is pulled back and the compound body as culturally constructed and as biologically real is exposed for examination.[5] Practices of dehumanization and the dwarfing of identity and meaning are noted, exposed, and dissected from a variety of vantage points. In this four-panel painting the bodies don't dance; they are stationary (yet floating) with more organs exposed than one finds with 'Flexible' (1984). Yet, these stationary bodies remain subject to dehumanization, to manipulation through exposure, as their organs presented to viewers suggest. They are pulled apart, rendered accessible to the gaze.

In 'Grillo', the body in the far left panel is tall and takes up the full frame. Arms are not present, nor are legs discernible. Furthermore, while the connection is vague at best, there is something that resembles a tray, perhaps with drinks, that is almost connected to the right shoulder by means of an orange line. This body might be understood to be in service, that is, it seemingly provides something to the viewer. The digestive system, including the stomach, is highlighted, all colored yellow, with touches of red. Although there are no pupils, the eyes capture the viewer's attention because of their bright yellow centers. The nose is red and pronounced and the mouth is open, running the full width of the face. The mouth is red with jagged teeth fully exposed.

Above the head of the body on the right (two panels to the right of the image with a tray) is a crown—a common element in Basquiat's paintings that might speak to majesty, to royalty or, as some have argued, simply point to his viewing of the television program *Little Rascals* (Thompson 1992, 28–42). One eye is yellow and the other orange, oblong in shape and piercing. There is the faint outline of arms with orange balls that could constitute fists. Within the rectangular body, the throat, lungs, stomach, and intestines are evident. There is a black box where legs could be. This body seems aggressive, in protest and confronting the viewer. The two bodies provide a sense of how black bodies are positioned: in service (to the system) and in protest (against the system). One might consider this a form of double consciousness. Both bodies are opened to view because the organs are exposed. Over against these bodies is a mostly white background with signs, symbols, and words drawn from the cultural worlds defining the nature and meaning of embodied blackness.

Between the two bodies are two panels. One panel is green with two white squares framed in gold, one of which has an image of a black head with white eyes. As part of this same panel, there is a large building marked up and partially hidden by gold lines and white slashes. A large "R" is crossed out by means of a box with vertical and diagonal lines and below it are words partially hidden; the third word might be racism. An empty square is below the four partially visible words. Attached on the opposite side, near the bottom of the building, are two pieces of paper; one with a movie camera and the words "film camera" below it and the other is a drawing with the word "agitate". The other panel has a green background that partially hides numerous images by means of quickly applied yellow paint. Some gold paint marking out three geometrical shapes contrasts against the yellow in a way that draws one's attention.

If one looks at the four-panel work from right to left or left to right, the panels without the symbols provide something of a brief break from the intensity of the bodies exposed. This is an opportunity to adjust vision, think about what has been seen, before moving on to what the next embodied body exposes to the viewer. The bodies are exaggerated, shifted in form, but still recognizable; the words, signs, and symbols surrounding them only add to their substantive presence and recognition through distinction. The figures are constructed in a rather simple way; to be sure, they are bare in more than one way. The words are intense, telling stories. Or, as Robert Farris Thompson remarks, "texts in his paintings are, among many things, brave essays in cultural self-definition" (Thompson 1993, 28). It is as if there is no distinction between word, symbol, sign, organs, and body in that each and all tell the same story of cultural worlds encountered. What can the body do and be without organs exposed, with signs and symbols all around impinging on the body—shaping its space and guiding perception?

Basquiat's personal history runs through a larger history of literacy denied, of signs and symbols working against embodied black bodies in an effort to control and place them, and to fix them in space. His use of words, signs, and symbols functions to seize language and make it function differently—to no longer hide but reveal information. The body is pulled apart and the words and signs that typically exist out of view are exposed, and through this exposure Basquiat brings the cultural codes and social trappings that shape the parameters of existence into view. "Basquiat", writes Klaus Kertess, "was a composer of oral/visual incantations that chant out the joys and tribulations of the invention of his self and his art and of that art's identification with the joys and tribulations of the disenfranchised" (Kertess 1993, 50). In pieces such as 'Grillo' and 'Flexible' Basquiat presents a visual history lesson, one that pulls readers across centuries, through various geographies (Saggese 2014, 42-3). These paintings position the body as without certain markers of social significance, which is rather unusual if we consider Basquiat's oeuvre. But there is more to it than this. Social markers are removed but the manner in which these bodies are embodied remains available for observation. These aren't corpses; rather, they are more along the lines of an embodied cartography of survival within a context of disregard, exposing their vitality (organs) so as to make the survival of the black body that much more pronounced, that much more a signifying of cultural narratives of disregard. The signifiers meant to capture and name black bodies are stripped away. Those are now outside the body, exposed. The mechanics that manage the workings of the body as it occupies time and space are also exposed. Ontology is a messy business as it brushes up against embodied history and its system of engagements, transforming this history while being transformed by it. By removing the "stuff" that limits the arrangement and meaning of black life, it might be said Basquiat exposes the humanity of African Americans.

ENDING THE CHAPTER ON A RELIGIOUS NOTE

When viewing the images discussed here, there is a desire—an urge really—to clean up the space marked out. There is a desire to put things in order so as to make their meaning straightforward and clear. This is a response to absurdity that frames the construction of bodies, the knee-jerk desire to fix contradiction and epistemological and ontological disorder. But it is important to note that this effort to fix should not happen. To order this representation of the body, the compound black body, is to play into the cultural status quo that seeks to shape these bodies simplistically. The recognition of the impact of racialization is to maintain the tension, to accept the paradox and existential "mess".[6]

The individual, the figure exposed, is connected to markers representing the presence of others, the signs and symbols of cultural language and, hence, to a dimension of life. Bodies always inhabit the world in the context of others, no matter how vaguely represented. The viewer of Basquiat's work, then, is connected to the cultural world represented by and through the piece of art. In its roughness, the rugged depiction, there exists something of deep value to those open to/for the search. All this speaks to the chaotic nature of life, the complexities of the existential arrangements that mark African Americans as fully human, with complex identities and desires for metaphysical markers of meaning.

Pulling together a variety of ontological and epistemological concerns is significant here. The "desire to visualize something racial and cultural", notes Powell, "yet also conceptual and metaphysical, found the ideal subject in black religion" (Powell 1997, 159). In this volume, religion is pushed beyond the typical terrain of doctrines and creeds and concerns instead a quest for complex subjectivity that involves probing historical experience for markers of meaning. As is evident through the images and words he employs, Basquiat's art reflects traditional modalities of the religious drawn from his personal history and the religious landscape of New York, such as voodoo. But there is also another sense of the religious at work in 'Grillo' and 'Flexible'. This other sense of the religious has to do with a more general desire (unfulfilled) to re-present meaning culled from the ordinary experiences that shape human movement through the world. It is a modality of the religious found within the body as the body presents itself and is presented. Religion here involves a method of interrogation, a way of exploring and interpreting human experience so as to track what we have come to understand as meaning. Thinking about this sense of religion, then, as a quest for complex subjectivity, this chapter revolved around two questions: In what ways does African American visual art signify dominant western constructions of meaning through an appropriation of the body? And, what is the importance of the body artistically reconstructed? In the rest of this section, as we continue our exploration of body *and* religion by engaging African American cultural production, we will attempt to offer additional answers to these questions. Engaging literature, film, and Black Greek Letter Organizations, we will explore the ways in which black bodies move through and navigate the world in a search for meaning, thereby challenging and transcending the social constructs that are tied to their race and gender.

NOTES

1 One could wrestle with Basquiat's representation of the body using Gilles Deleuze's notion of the body without organs (1969). That would be an intriguing discussion. However, for the purposes of this chapter, a more subtle application of *a*theology, philosophy of art, art criticism, and existentialism (particularly the moralism of Albert Camus) is more appropriate.
2 Perhaps these bodies show at least one sign of his home—New York City—that during the 1980s experienced the rock shaped death called crack cocaine. Cheap and deadly, it changed the body, mutated its form, and blurred its graphic beauty.
3 Basquiat, *Flexible* image, 1984. Available from: http://www.bing.com/images/search?q=basquiat+%22Flexible%22++1984&view=detailv2&&id=15731AD9CDCB77AF55AE2BC94B1794B9840DBFB6&selectedIndex=0&ccid=pI6kXJEf&simid=608038112735330665&thid=JN.Ffei889OZret4Lf5MpE%2beQ&ajaxhist=0 (accessed August 18, 2016).
4 Basquiat, *Grillo* image, 1984. Available from: http://www.bing.com/images/search?q=grillo+1984+basquiat&view=detailv2&&id=A26EBC13224E49E9F-140D5860E4C80A839E704DC&selectedIndex=0&ccid=%2ba9ZttFw&simid=608033405456155333&thid=JN.lbJ2XTtFo3NT5nFrwJ4jNg&ajaxhist=0 (accessed August 18, 2016).
5 In some of his drawings/paintings, body parts are presented without bodies—just organs exposed to view.
6 For an interesting take on the function of race in Basquiat's work see Saggese (2014: ch. 1).

Chapter Four

Unchained Bodies: Black Womanhood, Resistance, and Complex Subjectivity in Black Literature

> Here, in this here place, we flesh; flesh that weeps laughs; flesh that dances on bare feet in the grass. Love it. Love it hard.
>
> (Morrison 1987, 88)

In May 2016 cartoonist Ben Garrison posted a cartoon to Twitter depicting Presidential candidate Donald Trump's wife, Melania, and First Lady Michelle Obama side by side. The First Lady is depicted in a green dress with masculine features, muscles, and a bulge as if she has a penis. In contrast, Melania Trump is portrayed in a pageant gown holding a Trump sign and a caption that says "Make the first lady great again" (*Daily Mail* 2016). This image shows that representations of black women, in particular their bodies, continue to be problematic. That is, black women continue to be rendered in dehumanizing ways that seek to undermine their femininity by rendering them masculine, sexually deviant, or asexual. In order to resist this, black women have come to define femininity for themselves by making their own lived experience—rather than the ideals of white society—the measuring stick. As a result, black women often perform gender in ways that are considered non-normative. Here, we understand such acts as part of a quest for complex subjectivity, an effort to hold in tension multiple ontological possibilities for defining oneself as a black woman (Pinn 2003, 158). In defining for oneself what it means to be both black and female, African American women resist structures of cultural domination and fixed gender markers. This, in turn, allows them to assert themselves as subjects and purveyors of cultural meaning.

In this chapter, we will explore this by turning to Toni Morrison's *Beloved* (1987) and Octavia Butler's *Wild Seed* (1980), which discursively render the quest for complex subjectivity by portraying black female bodies that, in their gender fluidity, resist being controlled by oppressive forces and structures. In *Wild Seed*, the protagonist transforms into a male body to assert her freedom, all the while continuing to identify as a black woman. This shapeshifting, we suggest, is a literary rendering of the ways in which lived black female experience enforces different means of resisting the terror of fixed identity and thereby allows for a myriad of ways of becoming active subjects. Moreover, in shapeshifting, Butler's protagonist subverts her male counterparts and acts in ways that are considered to be threatening to masculinity and male dominance. Subsequently, *Beloved* will further illustrate our point by offering a framework for, to use Alice Walker's famous words, "loving oneself regardless"—which is to say, for asserting the value of black femininity and humanity in the face of the dehumanizing and objectifying realities of slavery. Importantly for our argument, Morrison posits the black female body as locus for asserting the complexities and possibilities that mark black life.

In Chapter 3, we suggested that visual arts offered a window into black life; here we contend that black literature can perform the same function. It is in this sense that James Baldwin spoke of literature as a "witness" (Baldwin 1962). As a resource for the study of religion, it offers glimpses into situations showing ways in which black bodies navigate the world and respond to various modes of oppression. Novels written by or featuring black women depict ways in which African American women have responded to and challenged dominant structures, defining themselves as fully human in the process. In *Black Womanist Ethics*, Katie G. Cannon argues that black women's literary tradition is the best source for understanding the ethics that black women have created and cultivated in the face of sexual, economic, and racial oppression in American society (Cannon 2006, 90). As the black female literary tradition is tied to the first arrival of enslaved Africans, Cannon argues that black women's literature offers a glimpse of black life that can be traced back to the arrival of the first black bodies that survived the Middle Passage.

LOVING HERSELF REGARDLESS: WALKER'S WOMANIST DEFINITION AND COMPLEX SUBJECTIVITY

Alice Walker's collection of essays titled *In Search of Our Mothers' Gardens* (1983) lays out a four-part definition, coining the now famous term "Womanism" (Walker 1983, xi–xii). Walker defines a womanist as a black woman who is serious, in the sense that she takes responsibility for herself and her life, but also exhibits "outrageous, audacious, courageous or *willful* behavior" (Walker 1983, xi). Moreover, Walker argues that she acts as an adult, thereby countering the white tendency to refer to black people as "girl" or "boy". She further states that a womanist is a "woman who loves other women, sexually and/or non-sexually. Appreciates and prefers women's culture, women's emotional flexibility (values tears as natural counterbalance of laughter), and women's strength. Sometimes loves individual men, sexually and/or non-sexually. Committed to survival and wholeness of entire people, male *and* female" (p. xi). Walker's framework depicts black female opposition to narrow and fixed ways of being: to be "womanish" is to possess a bold personality. This is in contrast to the docility of Victorian womanhood, which has often been held up as a normative ideal of and for (white) femininity. Walker argues that a black woman should be "in charge". Black women balance the reality of sorrow and pain with the necessity for joy and laughter and are understood as showing concern for both self and community. But, above all, a womanist is a woman who "Loves herself. *Regardless*" (p. xii). In sum, a womanist both realizes that she is a subject residing at the intersection of multiple realities, and works to assert that truth as she navigates the world. Walker's definition of womanism locates womanhood on a spectrum, leaving room for a myriad of ways to be a woman—and, to be sure, an active subject.

As mentioned earlier, complex subjectivity entails the desire to become a complex conveyor of cultural meaning (Pinn 2003, 158). Put another way: human beings seek to define an identity that mirrors their lived experiences and social realities. African Americans have long struggled against being conceived as objects acted upon by dominating forces. Yet, enslaved black people consistently found ways to assert the value of their body, expressing their embodied capacity for desire and pleasure. While Pinn conceives of complex subjectivity in a way that cuts across gender lines, Walker's definition of womanism offers a more pointed line of reasoning with respect to her particular attention to the lives of black women. She lays out practical ways in which one might assert subjectivity, in the context of the specific cultural inheritances and circumstances, as well as historical and social realities, of black *women*. Her definition emphasizes that black women are not monolithic, and that there are particular embodied struggles entailed by the intersection of race and gender.

In this chapter, we examine how Butler's and Morrison's literary constructions of black female characters take up different ways of defining what it means to be black women. These black women characters are combating the terror of fixed identity with the tools that Walker alludes to in her definition of womanism. Both women, we argue, opt for their own survival and love themselves... Regardless.

RENDERING BLACK WOMEN'S BODIES: GENDER PERFORMANCE AND RESISTANCE

Ever since slavery, when black women were forced to perform tasks that were usually performed by men, masculine traits have been attributed to black women (Cannon 2006, 31). The notion that black women possess inordinate, superhuman strength has, subsequently, found its way into stereotypical ideas about black womanhood.[1] As such, black women are often thought and portrayed as performing gender in a way that lacks normative feminine traits and, therefore, are denied the status of womanhood. The Garrison cartoon cited above shows that such tropes and stereotypes continue to be invoked in contemporary representations of black women.

Black women's lived experience has long been overshadowed by tropes that have defined who they are in narrow and restrictive ways that therefore skew the realities of how black women might self-identify. This was the case as early as the antebellum period. Through being exploited and devalued, and conceived as chattel, their humanity was denied. Moreover, enslaved black women were seen as sexual property, often forced to nurse the children of their mistresses, and treated as "breeders" who, while divested of value themselves, nonetheless labored (in all senses of the word) to produce surplus value in the form of an ever-multiplying source of human capital (Spillers 1987, 68).

At the same time, white women were considered to be the pinnacle of femininity (Williams 1993, 60–1). Womanhood was associated with whiteness precisely because black bodies were discursively constructed as non-human and lascivious. Here, we are particularly concerned with the "Mammy" and "Sapphire" or "Strong Black Woman" tropes. In the case of the Garrison cartoon, the (former) First Lady does not fit into the Mammy trope, as she is not portrayed as the overweight, asexual, and comforting black woman that we find in the caricature Aunt Jemima or that resembles Mammy in the film *Gone with the Wind* (1939). She is depicted as Sapphire: the hyper-independent, strong, and emasculating black woman. This persona is exaggerated further by the bulge in her dress. She is not considered to be the "portrait" or ideal of true womanhood. Patricia Hill Collins argues that depictions of this sort constitute "controlling images", which "are designed to make racism, sexism, poverty, and other forms of social injustice appear to be natural, normal, and inevitable parts of everyday life" (Collins 2000, 69). As such, these tropes help to justify black women's oppression because they strip them of individual identities and divest them of the traits of normative womanhood. This renders black women as either domesticated or deviant; in both cases, they are devoid of humanity and femininity.

Again, the way Michelle Obama is portrayed stands in stark contrast to Melania Trump who is depicted as the epitome of femininity, fitting into classic patriarchal gender roles. Though she attended college, where she studied architecture, she is also a former model and jewelry designer who is largely overshadowed by her husband, and considered submissive to him. In contrast to Ms. Obama, Ms. Trump is portrayed in the cartoon as the hope for a better and classier First Lady, a beacon of "true womanhood". Or, with a playful nod to her husband's campaign slogan, "Make the First Lady Great Again". These stereotypical depictions are an example of black women's longstanding experience with what Pinn calls the "terror of fixed identity" (Pinn 2003, 175). White supremacist ideologies continue to assign identities to black women that do not represent their lived experiences. Black women's struggles to assert themselves as active and independent subjects pose a challenge to white patriarchal gender norms that render a woman's identity subordinate to men. These social norms relegate black women to a second-class status; in response, black women continue to struggle against being demeaned and defined by patriarchy and white supremacy.

In defining womanhood in a way that mirrors their particular experiences, black women have often had to take on supposedly "masculine" traits or tasks; yet this need not be seen as undermining their femininity. Instead, these practices demonstrate that gender performances fall on a wide spectrum for which the normative male/female binary is inadequate. By performing what Judith Halberstam (2004) calls "female masculinity", black women subvert gender norms and thereby undermine the power structures that depend upon those norms. Halberstam argues that gender is constructed so that there are simple binaries (i.e., male/female) that are conducive to patriarchal power structures that punish deviations from normative gender prescriptions. Masculinity as a social construction affects everyone, as it marks hierarchies of power and privilege. Halberstam writes, "masculinity in this society inevitably conjures up notions of power and legitimacy and privilege; it often symbolically refers to power of the state and to uneven distributions of wealth" (Halberstam

2004, 2). It also determines what is considered "not masculine", bifurcating manliness over and against the "feminine". Sustained performances of "masculine" traits by women therefore threaten to destabilize this binary. Thus, dehumanizing representations of these women should be seen as ways in which this patriarchal power structure attempts to protect itself from such threats by punishing acts of destabilizing "deviance".

Halberstam's argument is compelling, yet she does not fully consider how embodied racial identity interacts or intersects with her concept of "masculine femininity". For black women, such fluidity in gender has historically been common due to, as discussed above, the ways masculine traits have historically been assigned to black women's bodies. We see a literal rendering of this in *Wild Seed*: Octavia Butler's protagonist calls attention to the existence of a spectrum of gender performances through shifting between male and female—and black and white—bodies and identities. As we will see, by altering her physical body Butler's protagonist undermines structures of power with regard to race and gender.

DANGEROUS BODIES: GENDER PERFORMANCE AND RESISTANCE IN WILD SEED

Anyanwu, the protagonist in *Wild Seed*, defines herself as a black (African) woman, yet she performs both genders. Such fluidity and shapeshifting is part of her daily reality, and allows her to exercise subjectivity in the face of varying forms of oppression. When Doro, a one thousand year-old being that possesses the bodies of others, finds her, she has already walked the Earth for three centuries, lived through multiple wars, many marriages, and outlived many of her children. When Anyanwu learns that Doro assumes the bodies of women she assesses his ability to act like a woman: "But...you would make a bad woman however you looked. I would not want to see you as a woman" (p. 92). This seems to suggest that Doro does not "perform" gender, but merely "assumes" female bodies. That is, even in female form, he can be identified as a male; Anyanwu, in contrast, knows how to assume and perform both genders so that when she transforms her body she *is* that gender physiologically and in performance. Doro does not consider her to be a man, despite her muscular frame. When he questions why she often moves about as a man she replies, "people will think before they attack a man—even a small man. And they will not become angry if a man gives them a beating" (p. 25). Anyanwu understands that gender norms dictate that the amount of strength that she possesses is threatening to maleness, and that taking any sort of female form opens her up to the threat of violence.

While not forcibly enslaved, Anyanwu is kept and controlled by Doro. Throughout the novel she is constantly struggling with being forced to bear Doro's and other men's children, her desire to protect her family and her growing hatred with being manipulated by Doro. She never submits to docility, but resists the constant attempts to force her into submission. For instance, when Doro forces her to marry his son Isaac, Anyanwu manipulates her reproductive system, which kills Isaac's sperm and prevents her from becoming pregnant. Butler writes: "Within her body, she killed his seed. She disconnected the two small tubes through which her own seed traveled to her womb. She had done this many times when she thought that she had given a man enough children. Now she did it to avoid giving any children at all, to avoid being used" (p. 114). This type of resistance to childbirth also alludes to the history of enslaved women who sometimes killed their own children so that they would not become slaves, as we will see shortly when we turn to *Beloved*.

Timmel Duchamp suggests that Anyanwu has a sort of powerlessness in her relationship with Doro, yet refuses to give up: "Since Anyanwu, like many of Butler's protagonists, cannot defeat her opponent, she is forced to choose between negotiating the conditions of her oppressive circumstances or suicide—and chooses, for important and interesting reasons, to negotiate with her oppressor" (Duchamp 2013, 87). Although she actively resists Doro's violent episodes, she also realizes that there is nothing that she can do that will sufficiently satisfy Doro: "after all of her submission, he still meant to kill her" (p. 163). This realization, coupled with the grief of losing her husband, drives her to transform into a bird, and then a dolphin, in order to escape. Survival takes on a drastically different shape than the one that she had lived in as a captive under Doro's manipulation. She is no longer concerned with whether he could or would kill her, or even with whether she can keep her progeny safe. She cannot ensure those circumstances, and when she realizes this, her own well-being becomes most important. Her love of self manifests in her escape from her captor, even though it meant leaving her descendants behind.

Anyanwu's ability to take on a male body is a source of fear and anxiety for Doro and other men. By being able to perform masculine characteristics, and even being able to produce children as a man, she subverts constructs of male supremacy. Normative masculinity considers the prospect of a spectrum of gender performance as problematic, and also deems female success without male interference threatening. Anyanwu's ability to literally be(come) masculine while continuing to define herself as a woman lends to a conflation of social constructions of gender. Walker's definition, moreover, helps us to understand how Butler's protagonist asserts a sense of self by choosing herself and her own survival when in the face of oppression. When Doro tracks Anyanwu down after she runs away from him, he finds that she is the owner of a plantation (Butler 2007, 196). Her plantation functions more like a compound that she manages with the help of close friends and family. She takes on the form of a white man in her interactions with neighbors and other outsiders in order to fit into the racist and patriarchal society without causing alarm that would likely bring violence to her and those that live on her compound. Taking note of how much she has flourished, Doro says, "Now, a century after I lost you, I find you young and well—greeting me as though we had just seen each other yesterday. I find you in competition with me, raising witches of your own" (p. 82). Her independence is an act of subversion because she assumes that which is considered to be a male role, that of an owner. While Anyanwu has merely cultivated a prosperous life for herself and her descendants, Doro interprets it as her attempting to outdo him and, indeed, her way of taking something from him. She is no longer only a perceived, but an actual threat to his power.

LOVING IT HARD: EMBRACING SELF AS AN ACT OF RESISTANCE

Reclaiming oneself is also a salient theme in Toni Morrison's *Beloved*, which is a fictional account of the life of Margaret Garner, a runaway slave woman who chose to murder her own child rather than allow the child to be captured and returned to a life of enslavement. Sethe, the protagonist in Morrison's fictional account, is haunted by the experience of slavery and killing her child, and due to this is alienated by her community. Yet, she also experiences moments in which she asserts herself as a subject, or to use Walker's language, someone who "loves herself regardless" (Walker 1983, xii). As she navigates being a freed slave, emotionally and physically tormented by her past, she also engages in the quest for complex subjectivity.

Regardless of the state of the female body (i.e., pregnancy, sickness, etc.), enslaved black women were expected to fulfill their workload. Their bodies were both physically and sexually brutalized, and circumscribed in such a way that intentionally erased their humanity. Black women were cast as sexually deviant in addition to being property, which made sexual exploitation acceptable (Cannon 2006, 36). Asserting one's agency was often met with dire consequences. When, in *Beloved*, Paul D first arrives at 124 Bluestone Rd, Sethe shares with him the consequences of asserting her voice in protest of physical and sexual abuse when she shows him her whipping scars that are shaped like a chokecherry tree. She recalls her experience of being brutalized by Mrs. Garner's sons while she was nursing her then infant daughter: "The boys came in there and took my milk. That's what they came in there for. Held me down and took it. I told Mrs. Garner on em [...] Them boys found out I told on em. Schoolteacher made one open my back, and it closed it made a tree. It grows there still" (Morrison 1987, 16–17).

When exposing her back precipitates her first sexual encounter with Paul D, Sethe considers the ramifications of acknowledging that her body has desires. She muses that she has not had room for this while enslaved: "Though she could remember desire, she had forgotten how it worked" (ibid.). For both she and Paul D, it had been so long that they could not recall the physical excitement and anxiousness entailed by sexually desiring another person. As a formerly enslaved woman, the expropriation of her sexuality had led her to repress the fact that she possesses complex emotions and needs; she was, in that context, merely a body that was acted upon. Up until the appearance of Paul D, sexual desire had not been part of her daily life as she fulfilled her role as mother and daughter in-law, and had to cope with the ghost of her dead baby haunting her home.

Being alienated from her sexual desires was just one aspect of her oppression. Denial of the ability to fully embody or express emotions and desires made any attempt to claim a sense of agency or subjectivity next to impossible for her in that such effort would be met with harsh reprisals. While Sethe's back is a physical reminder of the price paid for that kind of resistance, it is crucial to note that this *did not* deter her from running away for the sake of reuniting with her children, who had fled to Ohio. The escape from slavery in Kentucky to freedom in Ohio ravaged her pregnant body. Indeed, she would not have made it without the care of a wandering young white woman who happened to encounter Sethe while making her own way east to Boston. When they meet, Sethe's back was still freshly wounded and her feet were bloody and swollen from walking across rugged terrain. Her physical body is torn and broken.

Sethe, like countless other enslaved black people before and after her, had to figure out what it meant to embrace one's body and subjectivity after a lifetime of having one's personal claim upon both relentlessly denied. In a poignant and poetic sermon, Baby Suggs, Sethe's late mother-in-law, addresses precisely this challenge of embracing one's newly freed body and "laying down one's burdens", using language that ultimately helps Sethe to make peace with herself and to find some happiness within her own body (p. 88).

Unlike Sethe, Baby Suggs did not have to escape slavery. Her freedom had been purchased by her enterprising son Halle, who is Sethe's late husband. Baby Suggs is an unconventional preacher who offers a body-centered approach to life for the community of newly freed slaves. She draws crowds to an open field in the woods, aptly called "The Clearing". The sermon Baby Suggs delivers there speaks to the ways in which blacks assert subjectivity precisely through an embrace of their embodied flesh. She proclaims,

> Here, in this here place, we flesh; flesh that weeps, laughs; flesh that dances on bare feet in grass. Love it. Love it hard. Yonder they do not love your flesh. They despise it. They don't love your eye; they'd just as soon pick 'em out. No more do they love the skin on your back. Yonder they flay it. And O my people they do not love your hands. Those they only use, tie, bind, chop off and leave empty. Love your hands! Love them. Raise them up and kiss them. Touch others with them, pat them together, stroke them on your face 'cause they don't love that either. *You* got to love it, *you*! And all your inside parts that they'd just as soon slop for hogs, you got to love them. The dark, dark liver—love it, love it, and the beat and beating heart, love that too. More than lungs that have yet to draw free air. More than your life-holding womb and your life-giving private parts, hear me now, love your heart. For this is the prize. (Morrison 1987, 89)

Here, Baby Suggs proclaims the reality of the enslaved black body. It is despised and used as property. It is a commodity. As newly freed slaves, she suggests it is the individual's responsibility to love her or his physical body. She argues that it is vital to see oneself as valuable in spite of dehumanization. Though she is not speaking specifically to a crowd of women, she does employ some of the same motifs that we find in Walker's definition of womanism. Black people confront negative circumscriptions of their bodies by embracing those bodies. They accept the scars of slavery, but they offer love to all parts of their bodies and extend actions of love toward other black bodies. Baby Suggs claims that one must choose to embrace oneself and pursue one's happiness within one's body. In this moment, Sethe chooses (for) herself and pursues her own happiness, refusing to accept her forced alienation from the community for killing her child.

Though she is haunted by her past, one poignant moment when she minds Baby Suggs's advice to "lay it all down" and choose her own happiness occurs as she and her two girls ice-skate. Regarding this, Morrison writes: "Anybody feeling sorry for her, anybody wandering by to peep in and see how she was getting on (including Paul D) would discover that the woman junkheaped for the third time because she loved her children—that woman was sailing happily on a frozen creek" (p. 174). Sethe reflects on the nearly two decades she spent in isolation, grieving the baby daughter she chose to kill precisely to spare her from the brutality of enslavement. She chooses in that moment on the ice to embrace the decisions made. In doing so she is displaying Walker's womanish trait of willfulness. That is, she asserts a level of control over her own happiness and chooses herself over and against the perceptions that others in her community may have about her abilities as a woman and mother. The body, as noted, is central to this endeavor: in accepting her flesh, Sethe accepts herself.

Beloved and *Wild Seed* offer points of entry for discussing the ways in which black women define womanhood through asserting themselves as complex subjects. Both Sethe and Anyanwu are defined by situations in which they are divested of their agency through forms of enslavement, but they choose to embrace themselves and their interests. In assuming a male body but continuing to identify as female, and thereby performing both masculinity and femininity in unconventional and expansive ways, Anyanwu poses a threat to existing gender norms. The cultural tropes that reify black women as being outside of dominant social structures attempt to render black women's bodies docile. Yet, by continuing to perform gender in a variety of ways and define what it means to reside at the intersection of race and gender, black women question the binaries that preclude them from being considered whole. These exercises in the quest for complex subjectivity provide grounds for embodied experiences at the center of assertions of humanity.

In the next chapter, we continue to explore the ways in which black women have engaged the quest for complex subjectivity in and through modes of cultural production. However, while this chapter was primarily concerned with the ways in which black women subvert negative and dehumanizing stereotypes that render their identities fixed, Chapter 5 takes the topic further by arguing that Ava DuVernay's short silent film *The Door* portrays black female characters that just "are"—which entails the significance of ambiguity. In other words, while the quest for complex subjectivity is often understood as grounded in the terror or threat of a fixed identity, the responses vary.

NOTES

1 Collins (2000) and Wallace (1999) highlight the ways in which strength has become part of black women's perceived identity.

Chapter Five

It Was Written on Her Face: Religion and Black Women's Embodied Emotion in Film

Films bring bodies into view. More than that, as filmmaker and critic Leos Carax contends, bodies are central to the medium of the moving image, such that cinema *begins* with the human body (Kelsey 2012). That is, the very nature of cinematic story and its voyeuristic appeal to audiences hinges on the visual projection of bodies-in-action. As explained in the introduction, we understand the body as compound, that is, as a complex and continuous formation. Whereas the previous chapter primarily highlighted the discursive dimension, film offers us an opportunity to take a closer look at how physical bodies move, gesture, and are adorned—a project that we will continue in the next two chapters, when we discuss particular embodied practices in Black Greek Letter Organizations (Chapter 6) and everyday fashion practices (Chapter 7).

The body as depicted in film—whether walking, running, or making the slightest of gestures—can tell us something about the nature and meaning of human experience. Yet, the well-documented history of the objectification of black bodies in American cinema speaks to the way in which cinematic depictions of bodies-in-action are not constructed in a vacuum. From early silent movies, such as *Birth of a Nation* (1915), that solidified the association of black bodies with debasement and criminality, to the one-dimensional portrayals of black life in 1970s-era Blaxploitation films, the medium of motion picture has long been employed to visually constitute white racist ideologies concerning black bodies (Bogle 2001, 4).

The prevalence of objectifying black visual images has resulted in a particular kind of weight that is placed on black cultural production to alter and subvert such demeaning imagery through the creation of images that tell "the truth" about "authentic" black life (Fleetwood 2011, 3). For literary and cultural scholar Valerie Smith, these notions of truth and authenticity cited within black cinematic discourse have largely been synonymous with an emphasis on the projection of "positive" images of black life in film, such as those that cast black people as morally respectable and prosperous. In some cases, it also involves a reanimation and recoding of representational types previously conceived as "negative", such as the criminal or the buffoon (Smith 1997, 3). This chapter contributes to the discourse concerning black cinematic representation by considering as a case study the short silent film, *The Door*, directed by Ava DuVernay (2013).

DuVernay's film, we contend, is not so much concerned with projecting categorically positive or subversively negative images. Her project, rather, is one that eschews the confines of representational categorization—be it positive or negative—in favor of portraying rich complexity. More specifically, we argue that the film visually foregrounds the intricacies of black interiority through an embodied display of emotion and feeling by its black women characters as they confront and engage ideas of loss and relational connection. It is through the film's narrative dependency on bodily movement and gesture to convey a depth and dimensionality to black women's emotional lives that DuVernay provides a cinematic rendering of the quest for complex subjectivity.

DUVERNAY, THE L.A. REBELLION FILM MOVEMENT AND BLACK INTERIORITY ONSCREEN

Although Ava DuVernay has garnered Hollywood attention for directing the Oscar-nominated, big-budget film *Selma* (2014), her approach to filmmaking is grounded in her commitment to black independent film. She developed her filmmaking chops in this arena through two films, *This the Life* (2008), a documentary that chronicles an alternative hip hop movement in Los Angeles, and *I Will Follow* (2010), a feature film that depicts a day in the life of a black woman as she negotiates various relationships while grieving the death of an aunt. In 2012, DuVernay became the first African American woman to win the Best Director prize at the Sundance Film Festival for her second feature, *Middle of Nowhere* (2012), which chronicles a black woman's journey of self-discovery while facing the realities of her husband's incarceration.

DuVernay's work in the sphere of black independent film, however, extends beyond her own filmmaking. She also plays a role in the business side of black cinema through her production and distribution companies, Forward Movement and the African American Film Releasing Movement

(AFFRM). These ventures enable her to both support other black independent filmmakers in making their films as well as to distribute their films to wider audiences. For DuVernay, her work as a director, producer and distributer is a kind of call to action; it is a strategic effort to further black cinematic images in sustained and organized ways and without having to defer to the mainstream film industry in Hollywood, a system that is largely exclusionary and hostile to black filmmaking (Martin 2014, 57). Moreover, according to film scholar Michael T. Martin, DuVernay's efforts reflect her sense that black cinematic images have a social purpose; they have the capacity to render black humanity with complexity through cinematic genres beyond those to which black characters are typically relegated in mainstream Hollywood motion pictures (ibid.). DuVernay's comments about the persistent popularity, among black film spectators, of the images of black life in such films as *Love Jones* (1997) and *Love and Basketball* (2000)[1] further demonstrates this point: "We want to see ourselves as contemporary African American people. Like, maybe not period pieces all of the time. Maybe not, you know, always heightened comedy [...] you know, or heightened danger or violence. We just want to be. Just black folks being black folks—loving, living, losing" (The New School 2011).

The emphasis DuVernay places here on the need for cinematic images of African Americans "just being" is indicative of how her style of filmmaking is significantly informed by the cinematic approaches espoused by a cadre of filmmakers known as the L.A. Rebellion, or the Los Angeles School of Black Filmmakers. Comprised of a number of black film students attending the University of California, Los Angeles Film School in the late 1960s to late 1980s, members of the L.A. Rebellion collectively sought to engage in what they saw as the revolutionary act of humanizing black people onscreen (Field et al. 2015, 1). In particular, filmmakers such as Charles Burnett, Julie Dash, and Billy Woodberry broke from not only the norms and structures of classical Hollywood cinema, but also earlier generations of black filmmaking. Specifically, they depart from the early twentieth-century genre of the "race film" and its emphasis on black middle-class ideals as well as 1970s-era Blaxploitation films and their overrepresentation of sex and violence. In contrast to these genres, they employed experimental approaches to plot, setting, and character development to explore the internal lifeworlds of poor and working-class black people (Field et al. 2015, 46). Such an exploration involved, according to cinema and media studies scholar Samantha Sheppard, the onscreen projection of black people as thinking and feeling persons. Bodies, specifically portrayals of embodied emotion, were central to this projection (Sheppard 2015, 225).

Sheppard makes her observations based on a close analysis of the role of affect, particularly as it is expressed through embodiment and displays of emotions and feelings, in L.A. Rebellion films. She argues that filmmakers involved in the movement shared a common interest in representing not only the external living conditions of many black communities, such as urban blight and socio-political alienation, but also black emotional interiority. That is, their films provide a way to consider "how and why black people feel the way they feel about the spaces and places they inhabit" through cinematic renderings that reflect how emotion becomes embodied (Sheppard 2015, 229). For example, in Billy Woodberry's *Bless Their Little Hearts* (1983), a film that captures the fictitious Banks family as they navigate the race, gender, and class struggles that inform their lives in Los Angeles, certain cinematographic techniques are employed to capture an emotive subtext at work in the laboring body of the family matriarch, Andais (Sheppard 2015, 230–1). One of these cinematic moments is captured as Andais rides the bus home from her job. In the scene, the camera focuses on her hand as she holds the rail of the bus seat. Her grip and the slow rotation of her hand, Sheppard points out, foreground her pensive and exhausted emotional state. Andais's hands are the focal point of another scene in which she and her husband, Charlie, are in a heated argument over his infidelity. At one point during the scene, Andais tells Charlie to feel her hands. Sheppard reads this gesture as not only a mere symbol of her hard work; Andais is also challenging Charlie to physically touch and feel her body and, in so doing, to become aware of his own emotional disconnection and his indifference to her exhaustion and disillusionment (Sheppard 2015, 235). Through these and other scenes that focus on embodied emotion, the film provides visual renderings of black life from a unique vantage point. Instead of a film that is concerned with making hard-and-fast generalizations about who black people "are" or what they "do", Woodberry's film offers a meditation on the internal, complex dimensions of black ways of "just being" in the midst of social and political realities.

Though the L.A. Rebellion Film Movement predates DuVernay by a few decades, her work is marked by the movement's cinematic approach (she has acknowledged Dash and others as significant influences on her own filmmaking), particularly its emphasis on black interiority as expressed through the body. In turning now to an analysis of her short film, *The Door* (2013), we argue for the religious significance of DuVernay's cinematic focus on embodiment in her depictions of such interiority.

THE DOOR AS EMBODIED QUEST FOR COMPLEX SUBJECTIVITY

Our attention to the religious significance of embodiment in *The Door* is guided by our focus on religion as the quest for complex subjectivity. For Pinn (2003), black religion includes the myriad of ways that people engage in struggles for increased agency and fuller lives. As noted above, for African Americans, whose bodies have been systematically rendered objects under the dehumanizing control of oppressive forces, the struggle involves an embodied push away from such objectification in order to assert a sense of subjectivity that involves creative and multidimensional ways of being. Through its attention to religion's fundamental core, this conception is one that expands the study of black religion beyond the more traditional institutions and doctrinal forms that preoccupy much of black religious scholarship. Further, it lends itself to an exploration of the various spaces in which black people engage in complex ways of being; above, we already discussed the visual arts and literature as sites of meaning-making. DuVernay's *The Door* offers an additional space for exploring the nexus between the body *and* religion. As we will delineate in what follows, the film's depiction of the shifts and dimensions of black women's emotive lives through an emphasis on their facial expressions and bodily gestures cinematically renders the religious quest for complex subjectivity.

The Door is one of ten short films commissioned between 2012 and 2013 by Miuccia Prada for Miu Miu, a high-end women's clothing and accessory line. The films, which make up Miu Miu's film series entitled "Women's Tales", and feature clothing from the line, are a collaborative work between the fashion company and the women film directors who wrote and directed them. To be sure, there is a commercialized aspect to DuVernay's film. But despite the film's commercial appeal and, with that, particular assumptions around class mobility, DuVernay's cinematic technique is a useful frame of reference from which to consider the body *and* religion.

In particular, *The Door* is filmed without audible dialogue. Similar to the tradition of silent film, its plot unfolds primarily through music and, of interest to us, bodily gesture. Through cues received from the black women's bodies moving across the screen, it is evident that the film captures a main protagonist, played by Gabrielle Union, as she grieves a loss of some kind. Based on the images of a wedding ring on her finger as well as the scenes of her lying despondently on a couch alone that are periodically disrupted by other scenes of her smiling in a wedding dress, the loss most likely involves a romantic partner. Throughout the nine-minute film, three other black women show up at the front door of her home, each making their own effort to help her navigate her loss and grief. However, the plot's details remain somewhat incomplete throughout the film. The full character identities of each of the women and the nature of their relationship to the film's main protagonist are left unspecified. Some aspects of their respective embodied interactions with the protagonist have an amorous quality, while others read as platonic in nature. Also left without clear explanation are the details concerning how the protagonist's romantic relationship came to an end, whether by divorce, separation, death, or otherwise.

By leaving these details open and unspecified, the characters maintain an ambiguity that eludes the totalizing nature of discursive representational typologies that inform and limit how black women's material bodies are viewed onscreen. These typologies—that include not only the demeaning Mammy and Sapphire figures we reference in Chapter 4, but also the figures of the respectable, faithful mother and the successful, professional woman that are often projected in response to the prevalence of demeaning images—are all-encompassing characterizations. They are one-dimensional performative tropes that dictate what we see onscreen is all there is to know about a particular black woman character. In contrast, the intentional elusiveness displayed by DuVernay's characters resembles what theorist Daphne Brooks identifies as the nineteenth-century performative tradition of "spectacular opacity" among black women performers. That is, by withholding and, in some cases, leaving open certain character-defining details, the actresses in *The Door* enact a kind of defamiliarization that contests the reductive transparency so often imposed upon black bodies, particularly as they are rendered visually (Brooks 2006, 8). Although their actions on camera indicate some sense of who these women are, there persists an ambiguity about them that resists definitive characterization.

Defamiliarization that belies easy, fixed categorization is not all that is made possible through the opacity at work in *The Door*. In displacing the cinematic pressure points that are typically placed on plot and character identification, DuVernay relocates them within the embodied emotions exhibited by the characters. In other words, by alleviating some of the weight placed on black cinematic images to follow a particular plot line or to project a certain kind of representation, *The Door* brings black women "just being" into palpable view. This occurs through the focused attention DuVernay gives to what film scholar Murray Smith contends is the power of film to capture the emotive language of facial expression and subtle gesture, a language that is often obscured by audible speaking (Smith 2010, 261). Although facial expressions and gestures do not reveal everything about a character, he contends, they do provide some indication of a character's inward, felt state of being (ibid.). This is significant for our interpretation of DuVernay's film, such that the camera's lingering focus on the physical body, specifically the characters' facial expressions and gestures, reflect the emotive depth and dimensionality at work in their interior lives. Each visitor to the protagonist's door elicits a different set of embodied emotive performances from the protagonist, the combined effect of which renders the complexity and multidimensionality that are central to the quest for complex subjectivity.

It is through the embodied interaction between the protagonist and the first character to visit her, played by Adepero Oduye, that the film establishes the protagonist's emotional distress and brings it into full view. As the protagonist opens her front door, the camera focuses on Oduye's concern-riddled face and bodily gestures. With her head leaning forward, shoulders hunched, and eyebrows furrowed, she searches the face of the protagonist with her eyes, seemingly in futile hope of some indication that her instincts have it wrong, that the protagonist's emotive state and the circumstances surrounding her predicament are not as bad as the visitor senses they are. She is met with a prolonged and hard stare from the protagonist that abruptly dashes any such hope. The protagonist then backs away from the open door and returns to the couch. Resigned to the protagonist's distress, the visitor relaxes her shoulders, purses her lips, and walks over the threshold of the door and into the home. Once inside, the camera focuses on the visitor's face as she takes slow inventory of the dark house and the empty refrigerator. The scene concludes with the visitor joining the protagonist on the sofa where Union sits with her arm propped up on the cushion to cradle her head. The two exchange eye contact while the visitor caresses the protagonist's arm and removes disheveled hair from her face.

In this scene, DuVernay employs the bodies of her characters to render the first of many cinematic "bruising moments" in the film. This involves what Sheppard theorizes as an emotionally charged scene that reflects certain cultural narratives and memories that are specific to African American lived experiences. Moreover, these emotional black experiences are ones that have often been disavowed or distorted within flat, one-dimensional representations of black life in mainstream cinema (Sheppard 2015, 229). In this particular scene between the protagonist and her first visitor, the camera focuses on the protagonist's embodied, demonstrative signs of distress, along with the palpable care and concern displayed through her visitor's facial expressions and physical touch. These two framings of body language work together to produce a "bruising moment" that brings into view what Patricia Hill Collins has identified as black women's traditions of creating "safe space". According to Hill Collins, these spaces are often informal, organically crafted spaces that black women create among one another and beyond the institutional forces of domination that circumscribe their lives (Collins 2000, 102–3). Importantly, within these protected social spaces, black women "come to voice" by speaking freely and listening to one another (ibid.). And yet, while DuVernay's rendering of distress and vulnerability among black women characters reflects the notion of black women's safe space, it also nuances Hill Collins's concept. That is, rather than hinging primarily on a discursive process of speaking, the tradition of listening and "coming to voice" that occurs among the black women in this scene are fundamentally embodied engagements that say something about the interior, emotive capacities and states of being among the characters.

The interaction between the protagonist and her second visitor, played by Emayatzy Corinealdi, presents another emotionally charged moment involving an embodied expression of black women's interior states of being. Through this depiction, the film introduces a dimension to the protagonist's emotive capacity that extends beyond the distress she exhibited in previous scenes. After begrudgingly complying with her second visitor's efforts to convince her to get dressed and leave her home, the protagonist finds herself in the middle of a dance floor in a club. Her lips, which are tightly pressed together, match the stiffness of her bodily movements, suggesting that her mind remains preoccupied with her underlying anguish. But the more Corinealdi's character dances and gyrates against her, the more the protagonist's reserved stiffness gives way to rapid movement and playful facial expressions. At one point, she even breaks out into the characteristically sharp arm gestures that make up the dance move, "the robot". The cinematography eventually shifts into slow motion as the camera focuses in on her face. With her eyes closed, head tilted back, and a pleasurable grin forming across her face, she rocks back and forth in rhythm, her anguish seemingly giving way to an ecstatic state of bliss. Through a cinematic technique that foregrounds the body, DuVernay marks the protagonist's subtle emotional shifts and nuances. In so doing, she renders emotional depth in what could otherwise have been a predictable "girls night out" scene so ubiquitous to films with all-female characters.

Although her time on the dance floor elicits a sense of pleasure and catharsis that seems to relieve her anguish, the protagonist's embodied emotions during her time with a third black woman character, played by the musician Goapele, indicate a more complicated emotive state. After Goapele's character shows up at her door with tickets to her music concert, the protagonist consents to joining her at the show. As she stands among the crowd listening to Goapele's character belt out a ballad about love, the protagonist slightly grins as if to identify with the lyrics. Her grin fades a bit, however, and turns into a reflective gaze as a flashback image of her standing in a wedding gown and reaching her arm out, presumably to a lover who is cut out of the frame, disrupts the scene. As mentioned above, this wedding gown image is a recurrent one appearing throughout the film. DuVernay has noted that she employs this technique (disrupting a cinematic frame with another image) as a way to mark the fragmented memories of a particular character (Martin 2014, 82). Yet, this appearance of the wedding gown image is somewhat distinctive in that, unlike earlier appearances of the image in the film, this one is blurry. The camera returns to the protagonist's face as she slightly raises her eyebrows, returning back to herself in the present moment. She nods her head to the ballad and exchanges the blow of a kiss with her singing acquaintance who looks in her direction, as if sensing the protagonist's momentary flashback. This particular scene is one that complicates the protagonist's emotional trajectory to this point. While it would seem that she was able to shed her anguish on the dance floor in the previous scene, the embodied indications of her deep reflection here at the music concert suggest that she feels two emotions at once: even as the memory of unreciprocated love is beginning to somewhat fade, vestiges of its emotional sting remain palpable.

The emotionally-charged interactions that cinematically play out each time the protagonist opens her door to another visitor make varying embodied assertions concerning her interior state of being. From her anguished distress on the couch to her euphoric pleasure on the dance floor, and in expressions ranging from cathartic bliss to pensive reflectiveness, we gather that *The Door*'s protagonist is not a one-dimensional character. Rather, her shifting and unfolding embodied emotions throughout the film—that ultimately fail any attempt to pin her down according to preconceived representational categories—make *The Door* a cinematic rendering of the quest for complex subjectivity. And yet, the embodied emotions displayed by the protagonist alone are not the only way in which DuVernay's film dovetails with Pinn's theory of religion. According to Pinn, while the quest for complex subjectivity is concerned with individual expression and fulfillment, it is not a solitary or solely individualistic endeavor (Pinn 2003, 159). The push for complexity unfolds in the context of a wider web of social relations with other complex, multidimensional beings. This is significant for our reading of DuVernay's film in that the cinematic depiction of the protagonist's complex interior life does not come at the expense of one-dimensional characterizations of the rest of the black women characters in the film. The other characters both express emotions of their own and play an instrumental role in eliciting those of the protagonist. Although this is evident in the first three visitors discussed above who also display embodied emotions as they interact with the protagonist, this point is perhaps most compellingly clear through the protagonist's interaction with a fourth and final woman, played by Alfre Woodard, in the film.

Unlike her interactions with the other women, this one originates outside of the protagonist's home and is initiated by the protagonist herself. In this way, the scene signifies a striking shift in her interior state of being, such that it captures her move from acquiescently receiving her visitors' expressions of support to actively reaching out for support on her own. The scene opens with the protagonist taking off her sunglasses, uneasily biting her lip, and looking up to the balcony of a home where a woman, notably older than her previous interlocutors, is pruning plants. Sensing someone staring at her from below, the woman looks down, sees the protagonist, and makes eye contact with her for an extended period. Relaxing her shoulders and tilting her head with her lips pressed together, the woman's demeanor indicates familiarity and endearment. Without a word, she places her scissors down, removes her pruning gloves, and moves to join the protagonist below. The two women convene in an outside seating area where they engage in an inaudible conversation. The protagonist does most of the talking as she moves her arms and hands about to further communicate her point, presumably concerning the circumstances surrounding her loss and distress. The older woman, with her hand gently placed on the protagonist's knee, sits as silent witness to the protagonist's emotive release before offering what appears to be her own restorative commentary. Yet, the older woman's positioning up to this point as an all-knowing, wise woman figure is destabilized as she reaches to hug the protagonist. As the camera focuses on the older woman's face, her steady, measured demeanor gives way to a sense of uncertainty and vulnerability as she reflectively looks off into the distance, closes her eyes, and pulls the protagonist closer. But while the details of her momentary contemplation are never made clear, what is made evident through her interaction with the protagonist is that there exists for the elder woman a fuller, more complicated emotive life that includes, but also extends beyond, the wise, sharp-witted characterizations reserved for older black women characters.

CONCLUDING THOUGHTS

By the end of the film, the specifics of the plot and the identities of its characters remain somewhat murky. In the final scene, the protagonist sits at a vanity table where she thoughtfully removes her wedding ring. Then, rising from the table, she puts on stylish arm-length black gloves, grabs her purse and coat, and walks out of camera shot, presumably leaving her house. The lack of details here reinforces our contention that the film is not one that hinges primarily on the development of plot points. Rather, *The Door*'s cinematic emphasis and, importantly for us, its significance for black religion, rests on a rendering of the rich complexities, uncertainties, and fluctuations at work in black women's interior emotional lives. Such a depiction constitutes the black religious quest for complex subjectivity in that it continually outwits hard-and-fast representational categories, be they considered "positive" or "negative". Moreover, through the course of this outwitting, it also engages in the black religious endeavor to recast black bodies in creative, multidimensional ways. That is, similar to Basquiat's art work we discussed in Chapter 3—painted images that render the black body as undefined and ever-changing—DuVernay's cinematic focus on gesturing faces and bodily movement portray black bodies as repositories of boundless emotional depth and complicated feeling. In so doing, her film reflects the way in which the medium of the cinematic moving image, through its depiction of bodies-in-action, has the potential to function as an expression of black religion.

NOTES

1 These films are not directed by DuVernay. *Love Jones* (1997) was directed by Theodore Witcher and *Love and Basketball* (2000) was directed by Gina Prince-Blythewood.

Chapter Six

"School Daze": Embodiment and Meaning-making in Black Greek Letter Organizations

As we discussed in Chapter 5, film has been recognized as an important medium of black cultural expression for quite some time. And, in addition to serving as a vehicle for black expression, films often capture and preserve other modes and forms of black cultural production, such as Black Greek Letter Organizations (BGLOs), which will be our principal focus here.

In the late 1980s, one of the most admired films among African American moviegoers was *School Daze*, a musical comedy and drama written and directed by Spike Lee. Lee based the film, in part, on his experiences at Atlanta's Morehouse College.[1] In essence, the film is a story about black fraternity and sorority members who clash with other students at a fictional historically black college (HBCU) during homecoming weekend. Some of the themes that *School Daze* addresses resonate well with our discussion of body *and* religion. For instance, the film invokes issues related to colorism and hair texture bias within African American communities; it depicts models of campus activism; and it highlights some of the tensions that often swell between African Americans who attend colleges and those who reside in the nearby college towns—tensions that are often due to the former group's privilege and seeming disconnect from many of the everyday problems faced by the latter. Moreover, the film depicts the types of internal community struggles for meaning and identity that are part and parcel of the quest for complex subjectivity.

As this chapter will show, Black Greek Letter Organizations (BGLOs) are robust sites for investigations into how subjectivities are shaped by social and cultural arrangements. As we contend, whatever one labels—or points to—as an example of black religion it has at least one inescapable feature: it is a product of society and culture. In this chapter we will bolster this claim by portraying BGLOs as a type of religious organization. Moreover, we argue that BGLOs convincingly reveal why more sustained attention to the relationship between the body *and* religion is needed: bodies are central to how they, and any other organization deemed "religious", function as meaning-making entities.

TWO BODIES AND THE QUEST FOR COMPLEX SUBJECTIVITY

In this chapter, we focus our attention on BGLOs because they help to highlight the expansive influence of social systems on the attempted constructions of subjectivity we have been discussing throughout this book, and they do so in ways that push to expand our discussion of "compound"— that is, both material and discursive—bodies. That is, not only do social systems employ a variety of apparatuses that factor in the social construction of "discursive" bodies, but they also set the parameters within which material bodies engage in "liberative" practices. Accordingly, studying the embodiment of BGLOs will provide insights into some of the external social pressures on college campuses that influence their members' pursuit of meaningful lives through BGLO organizational structure. Moreover, BGLO members reflect some of the frustrations that arise due to the limited scope of Greek life as a "liberative" model. In brief, we contend that analyzing these dynamics within the context of BGLOs is useful for clarifying both how social environments shape the forms of subjectivity individuals take on, and how these environments inevitably limit the range of possibility for material expressions of meaning and the pursuit of more life options.

Our argument about the limits and parameters within which material bodies struggle for meaning in social systems is greatly influenced by cultural anthropologist Mary Douglas. Pinn's conceptualization of what we call the "compound" body is informed by Douglas; yet, we return to her specifically because she offers insights on the relationship between individual bodies and social systems (in our case, BGLOs). In her influential book *Natural Symbols* (1973), questions of embodiment ultimately relate to the work of individuals and collectives negotiating the strictures of social control. It is within the framework of such "controls", and how bodies participate in the negotiations of them, that the pith of Douglas's argument arises. As she puts it, "bodily control is an expression of social control" (p. 99). Hence, one's physical agency always points to various mechanisms that either open up or constrain the ways in which one navigates the social world and seeks for more expansive ontological possibilities within it.

Bodies are critical mediums of expression in this struggle—"natural symbols", as Douglas describes them—because they convey deep meanings about one's consent, authenticity, self-worth, and reservations in view of immense social pressures.

Douglas thinks of the interactions between bodies and social systems through what she conceptualizes as a "grid and group" interaction (pp. 77–92). A grid is representative of the larger social arrangement of ideas, practices, classifications, and symbols that establish "order", while the group represents various social relations where individual and collective bodies face overwhelming demands to clarify categories and provide orientations for common expression. Within this grid and group dynamic, "order" is the basic element of all communication, both verbal and non-verbal, as all of our social interactions require some semblance of order (p. 81). This is of critical importance to us here as we venture to discuss BGLOs *as* types of black religious expression. For now, however, it is sufficient to note that much of the complexity involved in black religious struggles—as embodied quests—relate to negotiating tensions between two bodies, what Douglas depicts as *society and the self*. This is because the "social body constrains the way the physical body is perceived. [And] the physical experience of the body, always modified by the social categories through which it is known, sustains a particular view of society" (p. 93).

TWO (MORE) BODIES AND THE EARLY TWENTIETH-CENTURY FORMING OF BGLOS

The history of BGLO formation gives important context to the frustrations inherent within the social arrangements that BGLOs must contest and emerge from as forms of self-expression. In fact, BGLO members' desire to match the social experiences of whites through Greek systems greatly affected how they employed their physical bodies toward that end in BGLOs' formation. This suggests something that is important to stress and analyze: BGLOs are limited within the controls and purviews of a larger white-dominated system of Greek social life.

In part, BGLOs are limited structures for black expression in that they share an important history of formation with white fraternities and sororities. In fact, looking at the early documents of both white and black Greek-letter organizations, one sees that they shared basic commitments to high standards of scholarship, the perpetuation of brotherhood and sisterhood, a striving for educational excellence, leadership development, and campus and community service. All of the social fraternities on college campuses—white and black—thus arose to fill a social vacuum. Through them students formed bonds that enabled escape from the tedium of class work and religious training. Furthermore, as historian Craig Torbeson (2010) notes, behavior not normally condoned—such as drinking, card playing, and singing—became institutionalized in these organizations and took on new meanings within the context of college campus environments (pp. 42-3).

BGLOs emerged during what Torbeson (2010) calls "the second wave establishment" of fraternities and sororities (1885-1929), at a time when the growing diversity on college campuses began to challenge the homogeneity of traditional Greek society composition. During that time, the typical college student was male, white, Protestant, and tended to be from higher socioeconomic ranks. White fraternities and sororities reflected this broader college composition, of course. Tensions began to brew on these campuses during this time. The increase of African Americans and other ethnic minorities, women, and Jews began to challenge the alienation and exclusiveness that these traditional fraternities and sororities represented (Torbeson 2010, 57-59). Consequently, it is understandable that African Americans would want to create their own fraternal and sororal organizations as well, especially on college campuses that were predominantly white institutions (PWIs) where, as late as 1927, there were only 1,500 black students (p. 60).

African Americans at PWIs were frequently discriminated against in every sphere of college life. In classrooms, they had limited interaction with whites; in athletics, they were not permitted to have physical contact with white teammates; and in broader collegiate social life, they were banned from joining any white societies or clubs. In short, as Torbeson puts it, "college administrations did nothing to encourage the socialization of their black students, and white students did everything within their power to exclude them" from gaining any type of enjoyment from college life in general (p. 60). One white society member during this time trenchantly captures the spirit of racial hostility, marginalization, and prohibition directed toward African Americans at this time in a recorded statement: "The presence of a colored man in our ranks would for many of us spoil utterly the social side of society life [...] Few of us would have been able to give him the glad hand of fellowship and social equality which would have been his due if admitted" (Wolters 1975, 319).

In order to foster socialization and feelings of belonging among black students who wanted to share in the advantages of collegiate Greek fraternal and sororal culture, black students had to form their own organizations.

Hence, BGLOs provided a structure for them to participate in a larger system of meaning that they considered valuable. It is helpful to keep in view our earlier discussions of complex subjectivity as a process of meaning-making. So, even given the obvious constraints, BGLOs compellingly exhibit a type of physical and kinetic creativity in response to questions of ontological and existential meaning that depict how black religion manifests in and as cultural production. BGLO embodiments would then become essential to ways in which some African American students solidify and represent their shared senses of identity in their pursuit of satisfying and meaningful lives. So much so that BGLOs became important structures for fostering belonging and meaning on HBCU campuses as well.

BGLO NATURAL SYMBOLS: BODILY AESTHETICS AND EMBODIED MOVEMENTS

Taking seriously the variety of meanings in black expressive cultures can illumine a range of socioeconomic, ecological, and political factors that provide context for understanding why and how African Americans attempt to carve out complex subjectivities. Yet it is important that scholars not ignore the physical, bodily artfulness entailed in such struggles for "more".

BGLO bodies are important aesthetic images in black expressive culture. That is to say, they are artful metaphors that influence collective imaginations about the nature and meaning of African American life within the context of higher education. Furthermore, as forms of aesthetic expression that can be "read", BGLO bodies—like religion—are products of culture. How BGLO members portray themselves has an effect on and maintains the construction of their realities (Berger 1990; Berger and Luckmann 1967). There are a range of bodily practices that are central to how BGLOs form group solidarity and self-understanding. Thus, BGLO bodies are ideal for analyzing as "location[s] for the arrangement and display of power" that produce "a certain 'art of the body'" (Pinn 2010, 10, emphasis added). Here Douglas (1973) offers a simple proposition about social structure and individual embodiment that helpfully augments this claim: "The scope of the body as a medium of expression is limited by controls exerted from the social system" (p. 98). Thinking of BGLO bodies as artful mediums for both expanding possibilities and limiting constraints is revealing for our analysis of black religion. Indeed, although BGLOs have a long history and record of involvement with social change and community service, they are also social bodies that are religious in nature because they arrange meaning and belonging for their members through inherited ideals and various modes of behavior and representations.

Two of the most prominent bodily practices among BGLOs are "branding" and "stepping". These bodily behaviors can be thought of as religious practices; they express a range of personal and communal meanings. In what follows, we examine these practices in order to uncover some of the fundamental desires members express through them. In addition, we will query these expressions for insight regarding some of the factors that also limit BGLO members' expression in college Greek systems.

BRANDING: PERSONAL MEANING-MAKING IN BGLOS

Attempts to historicize the exact origins of branding in BGLO fraternities are likely to be beset by problems. Like many secret order societies, these organizations are insular by nature, built on a foundation of hidden information only available to their members. Posey (2010) finds some public records from the fraternity Omega Psi Phi in her study that show members employing some form of the practice as early as 1931. Yet these same records also indicate that branding was "officially" eliminated in the same year (p. 277). A few states outlawed the practice, and most BGLO sanctioning bodies now disavow it, linking it to illegal abusive practices known as "hazing", which have increasingly received a considerable amount of negative public attention because they have needlessly resulted in permanent bodily and psychological injury or, in some cases, death to pledging members of fraternities and sororities. Beyond scant evidence, one would be hard-pressed to find members who actually possess knowledge of, or are willing to reveal any, official documentation regarding branding's ongoing history within their organizations.

In light of the public scrutiny and the repudiation of the practice by official fraternal statutes, Adam McKee, 1st Vice Grand Basileus (a key position within the central leadership) of Omega Psi Phi fraternity, stressed the idea that branding is not important to his identification as a "Que" and, really, should have no place in his fraternity. "I'm often amazed at some of the individuals that obtain or desire to obtain a brand [...] I've been in the fraternity many, many years. I am a student of history. And I often do research from the standpoint of the fraternity tradition and I see nothing in that history that speaks to or even alludes to branding as a procedure for the fraternity."[2] Given some of these more negative views, one will find that many BGLO members choose not to inscribe their flesh. Yet others continue to see branding as a consequential aspect of their Greek life experience. For these members, regardless of any negative connotations, the meanings they derive through this form of embodied symbolism is what is most important. As one member puts it, "People are always worrying about what happened a long time ago. What's going on now? That's what matters."[3]

The various meanings that BGLO members derive from branding are not at all static. BGLO members who do inscribe themselves come to see their bodies as effective tools by which they come to understand themselves and tell others who they are (Posey 2010). Branding is thus important because, as a ritual act, it participates in a new type of self-creation. Through branding, bodies have an altered utility: members employ their bodies in order to receive compliments, generate or reinforce their self-images, and transform the mundane. Several of these themes are also part of the stories we explored. Branding, for some members, then, is a significant aspect of the meaning-making character of these organizations. Unfortunately, there is not much available data on the practice among black sorority members, and readers will therefore notice that what follows are gendered, male-dominated accounts of these practices, which we acknowledge is a research gap that begs for further attention.

One of the salient themes one hears among BGLO fraternity members is that the brand tacitly conveys an "understood" identity. In other words, the brand signifies to others that one belongs to an exclusive black Greek-letter society and that one has further distinguished oneself by committing to a set of standards which makes them an asset for the broader black community (Posey 2010, 273). Branding shows a member has not only completed a set of difficult rites of passage, but has also undergone a final ritual of sorts—one that leaves a permanent marker of membership and devotion. One anonymous black fraternity member expressed this sentiment, noting: "I want everybody to know. I ain't got to say a word. They know what I stand for. They know what it's about."[4]

Other members claim branding is significant to them because the difficulty of the branding process itself engenders a sense of extreme value and personal esteem. Sandra Posey (2010) notes this holds particularly true for new members for whom branding is a way to demonstrate "deservedness" despite the fact that old pledge processes (including hazing) have been eliminated (p. 280). One of Posey's respondents said: "It's all about how hard did you pledge, you know how long did it take you to be made, you know, what did you go through. And for an individual now not to have a brand, it's like you didn't go through anything."⁵

Not all members would agree with such a view, but it is hard to ignore that some internal social pressures to be branded may jibe with membership post-authorized hazing culture—when "being made" takes on different connotations. In fact, some members would suggest the "pain" of the branding ritual is an important step in achieving manhood. Posey (2010) notes again how one member, Emil Hamberlin, conveys this thought:

> It's a third degree burn. It hurt. It hurt. It hurt. And the brothers in this fraternity, you know, we don't believe in one being intoxicated to numb the pain. No, no, no, you will be sober. You will take this pain [...] I went through a lot of things that were more painful, like having my shoulder dislocated, you know. But by me going through my pledge process of becoming an Omega man, I was used to pain. I was conditioned to pain. You know, I've learned to make pain my pleasure, so to say. You know, to look at pain as something temporary. To look at pain as something that has a time. It begins and it ends. Simple.⁶

The "pain" of "getting hit" is symbolized in the brand—and both the pain and the brand are given symbolic weight as markers of masculinity properly worn.

Some BGLO members attach important meanings to the specific placement of brands (Posey 2010, 275). Chest brands, for example, reference deep connections to the heart for fraternity members, and there are instances when fraternity members recount having brands placed on their arms, legs and butt to connote exclusiveness associated with belonging to what they call "ass" or "chest" clubs. There is an erotic understanding that can be assigned to the placement of brands on the body having an extreme character of "unusualness". Indeed, this erotic nature was portrayed in Spike Lee's *School Daze*: in a love scene, one of the actors discloses his hidden fraternity brand, which his girlfriend subsequently treats as an erogenous zone, suggesting that it has some type of sexual mystique. Furthermore, some respondents from Posey's (2010) sample claimed penile brands. One fraternity member described getting a penile brand on a "dare", and another mentioned he used his penile brand as a lure to pique a woman's curiosity. All of these brands—chest brands, "ass" brands, and the more exotic brands—are special category brands designated "legendary hits" by BGLO fraternity members. Whether or not these brands actually exist or not is less important than the stature one ascribes to the men who claim to have them, according to Posey (2010, 275).

There is no single, universal answer to the question of why a person acquires a brand. Brands may signify any number of associations for individual members—from personal achievement, to social ties, to aesthetic inclinations (Posey 2010). Yet, despite the intent behind branding, there are shared elements: ritual, ritual items, body, and body modification speaking to alteration of personal identity and meaning. This prompts a central question for this chapter: what does branding have to do with black religion? We argue branding can be said to represent the struggle to carve out multilayered understandings of the self. Through branding, African Americans on college campuses mitigate and reject notions of inferiority by insularity. While constrained and affected by the confines of Greek symbolic structure, BGLO members nevertheless utilize their bodies in ways to convey a certain specialness or chosen status—high standards of academic excellence and, in most cases, community service—which separates them from restrictive understandings of African American identity. In short, branding involves body modification intended to project a vibrant sense of self as a complex conveyer of meaning.

STEPPING: COMMUNAL MEANING-MAKING IN BGLOS

Another popular form of bodily symbolism among BGLOs is "stepping"—a community dance performance displaying various aspects of black cultural and Greek life. This practice was also highlighted, and actually first came to mainstream attention, in *School Daze*. Stepping combines songs, chants, and verbal calls with "precise and synchronized bodily movements that are stylized and percussive" (Branch 2010, 316–17). Although all BGLOs have their own distinctive forms of stepping, they share important similarities worth highlighting. As it relates to differences, for instance, the Alphas (of Alpha Phi Alpha) and the Omegas sometimes designate their style of stepping as "hopping", while the Kappas (of Kappa Alpha Psi) often name their performances "caning" (because of the red and white canes they carry). Yet, beneath all of these performances is a striking similarity: they demonstrate an important bodily "aesthetic of cool", as Robert Farris Thompson (2011) calls it, a bodily posture that pushes the range of acceptable expression. The "aesthetic of cool" is a tradition of embodiment that connects to the African continent, and, as Thompson describes, it is an "ability to be nonchalant at the right moment [...] an ability to reveal no emotion in situations where excitement and sentimentality are [usually] acceptable" (Thompson 1993, 41). In other words, it is the ability to act with an ease and austerity—their minds are in another world—while performing difficult tasks with a certain "air of ease and silent disdain" (Branch 2010, 324).

In these performances, BGLO members never let people see them at a disadvantage—their faces are stoic and their moves flow as if they are second nature. As Branch (2010) argues, because students of color face so many things beyond their control, the desire to keep themselves and their emotions in check during the show is particularly poignant. It is this aesthetic, this air, which gives certain flair while performing—all done with an expression of "grit" (Fine 2003, 40).[7] Carol Branch (2010), scholar of BGLO performance cultures, highlights the fundamental function of stepping for BGLOs: stepping "aids in maintaining the social cohesiveness of the BGLOs" (p. 316). As she sees it, stepping, much like branding, carries along with it the "complex histories, philosophies, and rebellions of its practitioners" (p. 316). And although it has become quite public on college campuses and in movies and YouTube videos, stepping also has private meanings attached to performance that most observers fail to grasp completely (ibid.).

Two aspects of stepping of importance for communal meaning-making among BGLOs are "circles" and "strolls". The circle, or the ring, is one of the more popular arrangements, and it has connections to similar practices in a variety of secret societies and social organizations—past and present. For instance, black slaves utilized the ring during religious services (Branch 2010; Raboteau 2004). According to Marcella McCoy (1998, 82), Africans and early African Americans understood that the circle is an arrangement that must not be broken; all who wish to pass the circle must walk around the formation. The circle also included counterclockwise movements influenced by cultural holdovers from the Congo. The counterclockwise circular movement of bodies symbolized the "circle of the sun about the earth" (Branch 2010; Raboteau 2004). Such historical and parallel practices aside, within the context of BGLOs, Elizabeth Fine (2003, 18) uncovered archival evidence suggesting the presence of the circle (or ring) as "the most commonly photographed pattern in the singing and stepping rituals of [BGLOs] in the 1960s". Still, for both BGLO members and those in earlier contexts, the circle, or ring, as Samuel Floyd (1995, 21) states, represents a "symbol of community, solidarity, affirmation, and catharsis". The significance of the circle carries over to the BGLO ritual called the "stroll". This is an informal style of line dance, "performed to music, where a group forms a line and performs a series of synchronized, stylized moves (steps) while moving forward, often weaving through other dancers and spectators as they go" (Branch 2010, 324). In essence, the stroll is tantamount to a smaller circle step. Audiences gather around the performers creating a large circle. However, if the stage or performance area—such as a party—does not allow for a full circle, the audience will form a half circle to view the event (Branch 2010). Again, we see members exhibiting a kind of cultural toughness or "grit" in stepping, which signifies to onlookers a type of personal development that is forged only through the secret rites of "brotherhood". Nonetheless, this more exclusive form of belonging is mitigated by the stroll and performance circles, which allow onlookers to participate. In environments shaped by a white dominated larger society, BGLO identity creates anew a black way of being that expands notions of blackness even as they mirror white mediums of expression.

CONCLUDING THOUGHTS: BGLOS AND THE STUDY OF BLACK RELIGION

Significant scholarship on black religion considers (at least implicitly) African American embodiment, focusing on how black American social institutions *reflect* salient issues of emancipation, enfranchisement, civil and human rights, and social and economic justice through traditional forms of religious expression (Baer and Singer 1992; Du Bois 1997; Edwards 2008; Lincoln and Mamiya 1990; Taylor et al. 2003). Yet less attention has been given to the inherent religious significance conveyed by the ways in which African Americans (re)arrange or physically alter themselves. Our work in the last chapter and the attention to BGLOs in this chapter is meant to offer a push toward greater consideration of body alteration and body manipulation as a component of the study of African American religion. In a word, attention to embodiment, or more "readings of black bodies" in various social systems, provides exciting possibilities by means of which to further uncover the nature and meaning of religion and its relationship to embodied bodies. Here we have argued for a reading that calls attention to body aesthetics and movement in view of Greek life.

NOTES

1 Morehouse College is part of a larger Atlanta University consortium that comprises other historically black colleges and universities (HBCUs), such as Spelman College and Clark Atlanta University.
2 Alan E. McKee interview with Sandra Posey, July 28, 1996 (published 2010).
3 Ibid.

4 Ibid.
5 Emil Hamberlin interview with Sandra Posey (2010).
6 Ibid.
7 Fine (2003) describes grit as "a characteristic expression displayed by pledges—a stern face with an out-thrust lower lip". Steppers often don this expression to show that they are serious about the performance.

Part Three

Religion in Everyday Life

Chapter Seven

Hoodies and Headwraps: Everyday Religion and the Dressing of Black Bodies

As they fall on a spectrum ranging from runway trends to workaday wardrobes, modes of dressing, grooming, and presenting the body are situated at the interstices of cultural production and everyday life; this chapter will, for that very reason, be the first of three on religion and the "mundane". As noted in the introduction, part of the argument of this text unfolds gradually and by way of the creation of three different parts: by moving from traditions, to forms of cultural productions, to, eventually, the mundane, we demonstrate that the category of religion should be expanded to include phenomena, people, and objects beyond and outside of religious traditions and organizations. The second section claimed that centralizing the body expands the category of religion in important ways, to include the works of Basquiat, Morrison, DuVernay, and Butler, and stepping and branding. This section furthers our argument by positing that religious meaning can also be found in the mundane, everyday aspects of embodied life. In turning to dress, food practices, and racial genetics, these chapters will help us to delve even deeper in the nexus between body *and* religion that we track in various ways in this book.

For our purposes, dress is an important topic to explore because it is, on one hand, a universal everyday experience that cannot be discussed apart from the body, and yet it is also deeply invested with personal, social, religious, and cultural meanings. By dress (along with fashion and related terms) we mean a category inclusive of not only clothing, but also grooming and related aspects of styling and bodily presentation. Because dress, so understood, always mediates the presentation of bodies, it becomes both a means by which embodied identity and subjectivity are socially circumscribed or "fixed", as well as a vehicle for individual self-expression, aesthetic affirmation, and the construction of religious meaning.

In this chapter, we will analyze case studies—from Trayvon Martin's hoodie to the conversations about transraciality spawned by Rachel Dolezal's headwraps—that foreground some ways in which everyday dress intersects with our exploration of embodied black religion. In line with the rest of the text, we understand the body here as "compound", that is, as a complex but continuous unit. And thus, we will focus on the ways in which the material body is always in some sense "dressed" (via markers of aesthetics, race, gender, etc.), and on how bodies are discursively constructed by various ways of interpreting and responding to the mundane practices of dress. This focus raises some preliminary questions. In what way does dress change how bodies are seen and interacted with, or how we feel and move with our own bodies? How are race, gender, and sexuality both related to and distinct from the various ways in which we dress our bodies? In what sense can everyday dress be seen as a religious phenomenon? In order to get the analytical tools we will need to unpack our case studies, we will begin by tackling some of these questions more directly.

(AD)DRESSING RACE, GENDER, AND SEXUALITY

Dress is a key way in which individuals present their bodies as aesthetically beautiful and/or physically comfortable. At the same time, it is an important index of how bodies are "read" or interpreted by society based on the ways in which dress factors into social norms and constructions of gender, ethnic identity, class, religious affiliation, and so on. For instance, imagine a marathon runner requesting a table at a five-star restaurant immediately after her race, without stopping to shower or change her clothes. In addition to receiving an awkward gaze from other restaurant patrons, she would likely be denied a table until she could comply with the restaurant's dress code. She would seem, as far as the social protocols of dress are concerned, to be as "out of place" here as she would be if she had run the marathon in formal attire.

However practical or even desirable social codes and norms for dress may seem in certain cases, they are nonetheless all cultural constructions that carry the same baggage as sociocultural norms writ large. In western cultures, for which white, male, heterosexual bodies are privileged as a normative ideal, "other" bodies that do not fit this description have had to come to terms with feeling and being seen as "out of place" even (and sometimes especially) when they are actually in accordance with other social norms of dress and bodily presentation. To illustrate, imagine now that our fine-dining marathon runner is a black woman, who, having already bathed and exchanged her running clothes for formal attire, now joins her lover for a romantic dinner. Let's also say that her lover in this case happens to be white—in fact, a white woman. Isn't it still rather easy to imagine curious or contemptuous gazes directed at the couple, or a certain feeling of being seen as "out of place"—even though with respect to the expectations of both the restaurant and societal fashion trends, the marathon runner is now properly dressed for the occasion? Although their bodies would be wearing the "right" clothes for this place and time, these same bodies are also "dressed" by their respective bodily markers of race, gender, and sexuality. Rather than violating social expectations about attire, in this scenario the couple bumps up against normative assumptions about race, interracial sexuality, sexual orientation, and perhaps even class, that may conspire to cause their sensation of being (seen as) "out of place" to linger.

We could then say that the body is "dressed" by its race and gender in the sense that the material body becomes the immediate referent for the various narratives, myths, stereotypes, and significations that are socially attached to race, gender, and sexuality. These myths and stories are woven or stitched together and then placed back upon the material body like a garment that cannot be taken off. That is to say, the ways in which individuals present and dress their bodies are never fully separable from the ways in which bodies are "dressed" by discourses of race, gender, and sexuality.[1] In this sense, dress is both bound up with, and serves as an effective metaphor for, the three intersecting "schemas" Frantz Fanon (1967) identifies in his existential analysis of black embodiment. First, he describes the "corporeal schema", which relates simply to the nature of having a human body—how it senses, moves, and interacts with objects in its world. This is well and good, argues Fanon, except that when one is racialized as black in an antiblack racist society, one encounters problems with this simple schema; one does not simply have a human body but a "black" body.

Fanon's second, "historico-racial", schema accounts for what this blackness signifies in a racist society. "Black" is not something a person intrinsically or essentially is (if all people had black skin, he argues, then nobody would be called black; likewise, in a non-racist society, being called "black" would not have the same consequences or connotations). Instead, "black"-ness is produced "by the other, the white man, who had woven me out of a thousand details, anecdotes, stories" (Fanon 1967, 111). Centuries of accumulated stereotypes, myths, anthropological and physiological treatises and travel accounts depicting black Africans as cannibalistic, hyper-sexual, demonic, cursed, unintelligent, subhuman, and so on *ad nauseum*, provide the various narrative threads that are woven together to constitute what Fanon aptly refers to as his "uniform" of black embodiment. For Fanon, challenging these damaging fictions about blackness is never quite as simple as merely debunking each of the myths and stories or rationally proving their falsity. This is because once the narratives are woven together and collapsed back onto his body in the form of this "uniform" they become what he calls a third, "racial epidermal schema". Here, there is no longer any need to explicitly state or reinforce the myths and stories because the "uniform" of black skin already signifies them. People simply react to him with an apparent automaticity that seems to preclude any and all mitigating factors: even though he is a philosopher and a practicing psychologist with a doctorate from a major European university he remains irrevocably black and hence "out of place" to the extent his body defies the norms and expectations society has for "blacks" as such.

In their discussion of African diaspora fashion subjectivity, Kaiser and McCullough (2010) help us to understand how Fanon's schemas intersect with fashion. They show how African Americans and their modes of dress have been entangled by dehumanizing narratives and targeted by disciplinary rules, laws, and codes that continue into the twenty-first century. One key example is the way in which the trend of sagging pants is not only targeted for social stigma and discipline, but is also framed in terms of several problematic narratives. They note that within popular discourse about sagging, there is a persistent desire to locate the trend's "real" historical origin in order to "pin down a precise and delimited subject position that removes the confusion, multiple meanings, and power of ambiguity" by asserting a single "authenticating narrative" (p. 370). While there is not enough evidence to finally reach such a settlement, the three most commonly proffered origin narratives pertain to slavery (not being given belts to prevent fast escape, or as used for sexual signaling), poverty (not being able to afford belts or properly sized clothes), or, perhaps most common of all, prison (belts as contraband, or again as used for sexual signaling). The functional effect of each of these narratives is to "entangle African American masculinity and criminality [...] to make sagging mean criminality or thuggishness" (p. 371). As these authenticating narratives begin to signify blackness as criminality, they provide a rationalization for a whole range of policing practices targeting both the style (in this case, sagging) and the populations considered to be associated with it: "In the process, popular discourses transform fashion subjectivity—and challenges to hegemonic fashion norms—into a rationalization for historical patterns of discrimination and fear" (ibid.). This would seem to be grist for Fanon's mill; the fact that many people who are perhaps not explicitly familiar with these origin narratives or myths would nevertheless have little difficulty associating young black men wearing sagging pants, or for our purposes a hoodie, with poverty and criminality shows how easily such narratives (the historico-racial schema) can be collapsed back on to the signifying skin, or in this case even cloth (the racial epidermal schema).

Our discussion so far has highlighted some of the problematic ways in which blackness is constructed as a negative signifier under an objectifying white gaze—the ways in which society uses dress as a way of "reading" discursively constructed bodies. However, it is equally important to emphasize that everyday dress is integral to the way individuals present and experience their bodies as aesthetically beautiful. To that end, Kaiser and McCullough's concept of black fashion subjectivity provides a helpful way of holding in tension the play, or as they put it the knots and entanglements, between discursive constructions attempting to pin down and constrain subjectivity and the ways in which individual fashion practices defy such constraints. That is, black fashion subjectivity is less about *what* is worn than *how* it is being worn, and entails "fluid, processual quests for meaning(s) through materials" in everyday practices of styling and presenting the body (p. 382). In this sense, articles of dress can take on a different meaning when worn by black bodies because they can create new dynamics of style—new ways in which the comportment of dress allows the body to move in and through the world conferring meaning, creativity, and pleasure. In other words, rather than conceptualizing the black body solely as inert—as "dressed" (passive voice) by blackness (signifying an ontologically "fixed" essence)—this framing foregrounds the agency and movement of bodies, the ways they carry, present, and, indeed, *fashion* themselves (in both a literal and figurative sense) in and through dress. Hence, we contend that fashion subjectivity should be seen as an important embodied aspect of black religion's fundamental impulse toward complex subjectivity.

As Monica L. Miller (2009, 3) argues, "stylin' out" is both a personal and political "performative act" that has historically been central to forms of black cultural expression. She contends that "when black people use the body as cultural capital and clothing as a necessary but unstable currency of self-worth [...] style reveals the value of blackness in a global market of identity formation in which, at different times and in different places, the cost of embodying or performing blackness can be both too cheap and too dear" (p. 25). This encapsulates the fundamental tension between restrictive discursive constructions of "dressed" black bodies and individuals' expressions of subjectivity and aesthetic value through dress. In the case studies that follow, we offer detailed analysis of these dynamics as they come into play in concrete situations.

HOODIES: TRAGIC TRANSUBSTANTIATION

On February 26, 2012, a Florida neighborhood watchman named George Zimmerman put in a 911 call about a "suspicious" looking character clothed in a "dark hoodie". Ignoring the dispatcher's request not to pursue, Zimmerman went after Trayvon Martin, a 17-year-old black boy on his way back home from the convenience store, resulting in an altercation that culminated with Zimmerman shooting Martin to death. One aspect that seems to set Martin's death apart from similar tragedies is the role that a seemingly inert article of clothing—a gray hooded sweatshirt—came to play in a story whose media coverage would at one point surpass that of the presidential election taking place the same year (Pew Research Center 2012). While conservative pundits such as Geraldo Rivera and Bill O'Reilly blamed the hoodie for Martin's death, others staged hoodie photographs, protests, and even a "Million Hoodie March" to challenge this narrative and express solidarity with Martin. So much was made of Martin's hoodie that in 2013, there were reports that the Smithsonian was interested in acquiring it for a display (Wemple 2013; Curry 2013; Lennard 2012).

In terms of our discussion above, we can say that while Martin wore his hoodie because of the way it facilitated his body's movement and comfort on a rainy day—and perhaps it had an aesthetic or stylistic appeal as well—these meanings were clearly at odds with the sense in which his hoodie-clad body appeared and was interpreted by others, particularly Zimmerman. For Zimmerman, and O'Reilly, Rivera, and other commentators, Martin's (fashion) subjectivity, along with his body and personhood, slip out of view, covered over by discursive constructions and authenticating narratives about his garment. From their vantage point it would seem that Martin ceased being a person and became simply a hoodie. On Fox News, Geraldo Rivera urged parents of black and Latino youth "to not let their children go out wearing hoodies", and suggested on his Twitter page that "a hood is like a sign: shoot or stop & frisk me", and Bill O'Reilly likewise argued that Martin died "because he looked a certain way and it wasn't based on skin color [...] he was wearing a hoodie and he looked [...] how 'gangstas' look" (Wemple 2013). If, for Fanon, the "racial epidermal schema" means that black skin has become so saturated with the negative myths about blacks that it now signifies all by itself, here we see that there is also a racial-textile schema in which it is clothed black skin that does the signifying. While Martin's shirt obviously did not actually have the words "shoot or stop & frisk me" emblazoned on it, it is equally clear that Rivera and O'Reilly harbored little doubt about its ability to signify, to communicate something that either justified his death or at least provided mitigating circumstances for Zimmerman's actions. Ascribing this degree of agency to an article of clothing allows agency and responsibility to be more easily disclaimed by others: Zimmerman can claim that the hoodie justified his decision to pursue Martin by making him look suspicious and dangerous, and media pundits and politicians can claim, as O'Reilly did, that "it wasn't based on skin color", even while arguing that it is because "he looked [...] how 'gangstas' look". In all cases, statements, policies, and actions that are racist in effect can be justified by purportedly targeting a garment rather than the black body underneath.

While many commentators were quick to point out that such obsession over a hoodie is as insane, insensitive, or inappropriate as talking about how "provocatively" a female rape victim may have been dressed before being violated, the fact remains that the way in which the victims of these crimes are dressed inevitably *does* become a key point of discussion in public discourse and courtroom argumentation alike. Why is this so? Has racism found a new tool in the form of a textile-racial schema that purports to yield usable and actionable knowledge about particular clothed bodies? Is there an assumption that the ways in which bodies are dressed in particular spaces and times communicates some concrete truth about them—that people wear their essence not only upon their skin but upon their dress as well? Do certain clothed, racialized, and/or gendered bodies really invite criminal sanction or sexual aggression? Just as one could dismissively argue that race is a social fiction rather than a biological fact, one could also dismiss the hoodie as an intrinsically meaningless article of clothing that had no real bearing on what happened to Martin. It could even be argued that focusing on the hoodie detracts from a genuine attempt to highlight the history (and the present) of victimized black bodies. But like Fanon's "uniform" of black skin, Martin's hoodie is also saturated with underlying narratives that account for its enduring significance to the discussion even in spite of such forceful dismissals. The hoodie, coupled with the black body, indeed does appear to produce a surplus of meaning with potentially lethal implications.

A purely semiotic approach to dress is inadequate here, because a hoodie can be read in any number of ways, including Zimmerman's problematic reading of "suspicious" and/or criminal. No amount of public debate or hoodie-clad demonstrations would suffice to make such a reading any less plausible to someone like Zimmerman. But this clearly does not mean that the ways in which dress is "read" are unimportant. While objects like hoodies cannot be intrinsically suspicious in themselves, they seem to gain this power to signify when aligned with some bodies, places, and times and not with others. It is within this particular context that articles of everyday dress like Martin's hoodie, much like our discussion of sagging pants above, gain the capacity, as Mimi Thi Nguyen (2015) contends, "to transform and render a body into being-as or being-like some other thing—the criminal" (p. 796).

While undoubtedly correct, describing the hoodie's role in terms of a transformation into the appearance of criminality does not seem to go far enough. Even if it transformed Martin's *appearance* into that of a criminal, this hardly explains how Zimmerman could kill him without being considered a murderer. In lieu of this, we suggest that what the discursive constructions of the hoodie performed might be better described as a kind of transubstantiation. In the Roman Catholic tradition, transubstantiation refers to the process by which the bread and wine of the Eucharist are (by way of an invisible divine mystery) transformed into the actual body and blood of Christ. The communal consumption of the Eucharist (like the practice of taking communion in other Christian denominations) is believed to perform the indemnifying function of (re)constituting the Church as the manifold "body of Christ", marked for eternal life by the blessings conferred by Jesus' sacrificial death (and resurrection). Here, we invoke this term as a way of highlighting an immaterial operation that purports to give material things a certain charge, or ascribe new meanings to them, for the express purpose of constituting and indemnifying a collective as "one body" that is marked for life and, by extension, providing an explanation (if not a justification) for why and how "other" bodies are marked for death.

In this case, the feat of transubstantiation performed by discourses about the hoodie converts the body of Trayvon Martin not (or not only) into the guise of a threatening criminal, but into a *thing*—an inert article of clothing. One cannot be held responsible for murdering a hoodie because it is an object devoid of rights and subjectivity. Thus, not only does the hoodie transfigure and mark Martin's body for legally sanctioned death, as well as provide coded language to cover the racial overtones of commentators like O'Reilly and the profiling tactics of the state, it also covers and reanimates the aggressor. That is, the hoodie also transubstantiates an aggressive perpetrator into a vulnerable victim who can then claim fear for his or her life. All too often the courts of both criminal law and public opinion uphold this magico-religious matrix by acquitting (or in many cases failing to even indict) the killer without questioning the automaticity, morality, or legality of his or her response. That is how George Zimmerman and the numerous other armed citizens, security guards, and law enforcement officers who have taken black life can defend themselves on the basis of "stand your ground" and self-defense even as they aggressively pursue and kill unarmed citizens. When reduced to the significations of his hoodie, Martin's death and Zimmerman's subsequent acquittal play out as a Eucharistic ritual that indemnifies the collective body of moral and legal responsibility. Martin's death would then seem to become a sacrificial legitimation of white supremacy's lingering effects on American social, political, and legal structures.

As a result, Martin's hoodie has elicited calls from within the black community urging youth to dress and comport their bodies with "respectability". This is proffered as a pragmatic way of avoiding situations, like Martin's, in which one's appearance and/or dress is cited as a contributing cause of violence or death. Aside from its clear pragmatic limitations, seen in cases in which even dressing and acting "respectfully" in accordance with societal norms does not prevent one from being violated, such arguments are also problematic in that they place strict limits on subjectivity: why should anyone violate extending their style of dress as self-articulation, thus denying or even erasing their subjectivity in order to appear nonthreatening, when even that cannot guarantee safety? Why violate yourself when doing so cannot guarantee against being violated by others? Furthermore, this reasoning seems to place the brunt of responsibility upon the fashion choices made by someone like Trayvon Martin while leaving unchallenged the assumption that folks such as Zimmerman (re)acted upon an automatic, involuntary impulse and therefore cannot be held criminally responsible for taking life. In a bizarre twist, the decision to put on a shirt is treated as the conscious choice of a moral agent whereas the decision to pursue and kill a teenager on the slightest hint of suspicion is rendered immune from moral, or at the very least legal, reprisal.

While we might wish to escape this tendency, there is an obstacle that is more than cloth and skin deep. Subjectivity seems to be constrained not only by a tendency to politicize a textile schema, but also by the operation of an underlying narrative or historico-racial schema that structures in advance the way in which black bodies are seen, read, and reacted to. Martin's hoodie clearly illustrates some of the ways in which everyday fashion subjectivity, as a component of a broader quest for complex subjectivity, becomes entangled in the interplay between expressions of individual agency and the ways in which society interprets and responds to them. Since the latter are constrained by the structuring construct of race, they impinge on the existential options of individual expression, and these consequences, as we have seen, can be deadly. Precisely for this reason, Pinn (2012, 63–4) emphasizes that the quest for complex subjectivity is not and never can be complete. That is, while one can challenge the terror of a fixed identity through, for instance, modes of dressing or grooming, one can never escape the threat that one's identity and body becomes, once more, fixed, objectified, and dehumanized. This is also to say that one never "has" complex subjectivity, because the push for more life meaning is always challenged, dismantled, and open for ever-new and constantly unfolding interpretations. While we have seen numerous examples of this push for and restriction of complex subjectivity throughout this text—think, for instance, back to *Wild Seed*, *Beloved*, and Basquiat's artwork—we encounter their lethal consequences in this chapter.

Dress entangles bodies within threads of subjectivity that simultaneously conceal and reveal, facilitating both recognition and misrecognition within a racial optics that is thoroughly enmeshed in power relations up to and including the power over life itself. For Trayvon Martin, a seemingly trivial, everyday choice of comfort and style was caught up within a web of signification he could neither have created nor conceived, and for the "crime" of being a "hooded" black body moving through a particular space and time, he paid the ultimate price. In the end, the hoodie's last act was to serve as a stand in for Trayvon himself, limiting the way we talk about and conceive of the value and meaning of his life to the conversations around the meaning of his death. In that sense, reducing the significance of his life to his status as a martyr for the cause of racial justice is almost as problematic as reducing him to the significations of his hoodie. Both maneuvers constrain his ontological possibilities in the fullness of life, and project those constraints onto those other hoodie-clad bodies that style themselves as his proxies-in-solidarity. The only difference would consist in what type of collective body Martin's death is deployed to sacrificially indemnify—either white supremacy or a purportedly more just multicultural society.[2] By making him into an "everyman", the stories we tell about Martin and his hoodie run the risk of subjecting his subjectivity, his individuality, and ultimately his personhood to the ontological fixity of a racializing narrative that at best instrumentalizes his death for a movement for justice, but at worst exploits it to reify the racial schema that (trans)fixed him as inherently criminal in the first place. What this illustrates, and what our second case study will further explore, is the slippage from social constructionist theories of race (i.e., race is a social fiction, not a biological fact) into tacit forms of essentialism (i.e., race as fixed ontological category) that can reinforce rather than challenge constraints on subjectivity—all within the context of everyday dress.

HEADWRAPS: TRANSRACIAL F(R)ICTIONS

We have already seen that dress mediates and encodes the presentation of the body in particular ways, sometimes by heightening the body's visibility or vulnerability and other times by obscuring it. We have also seen that this coding is imbricated in uneven power relations and social discourses of race, gender, and sexuality such that it facilitates both the recognition and misrecognition of bodies. In some cases, however, fashion subjects deliberately play on the (mis)readings that certain textile-corporeal combinations are subjected to in order to be intentionally (mis)recognized in particular ways. For instance, consider the way in which transgender people use the ability of cloth to render certain parts of the body invisible while heightening the visibility and readability of other parts in order to tap into the gender coding of dressed bodies and thereby present, perform, and/or "pass" as another sex. Former Olympic athlete Bruce Jenner made headlines in April 2015 by finessing this gender coding to come out as Caitlyn Jenner, a transgender woman. While transgender men and women had been engaging these fashion practices long before Jenner, her story is significant in that it brought the discussion of gender identity from the margins of culture (and arguably even the margins of the LGBTQ movement) into the mainstream of public discourse. It is also significant in that this conversation about the tensions and complexities of the body and its identity would serve as a key backdrop to frame the way in which another story about embodied "trans" identity would be discussed just a few weeks later.

In June 2015, reports began to surface about Rachel Dolezal, an adjunct instructor in Africana studies at Eastern Washington University and chapter president of the NAACP in Spokane, Washington. Like our first case study, this would turn out to be another instance in which the everyday dressing and presentation of a (supposedly) black body was catapulted into a media firestorm and a national conversation about race. Dolezal's fashions, and especially her kinked, braided, and head-wrapped hair, became national headlines and photo ops because her parents (both of whom are white) revealed that she had been lying about having a biracial identity. Amidst the media firestorm of shock, dismay, and outrage that Dolezal's racial passing generated, she continued to identify as black, claiming that for her racial identity is "fluid" rather than fixed, and that for her blackness is "not a costume" (Samuels 2015). Whereas Martin, as we saw, was victimized by the way his clothed body appeared and was interpreted, Dolezal seemed to consciously exploit the signifying capacities of her dressed body and the particular way in which body and cloth are brought together within a textile-racial schema. She knew that with a well-maintained tan, kinked, or braided hair, and elaborate cloth headwraps, she would simply be black as far as the world around her was concerned.

Like Caitlyn Jenner, Dolezal was keenly aware of the ways in which dressing, and in particular styling her hair, is coded by social narratives and assumptions about race and gender. Since both high-profile stories saturated the news media and popular discourse simultaneously, they were variously compared, contrasted, celebrated, and critiqued in tandem.[3] Though the term "transracial" had already been used to describe the experiences of individuals who had been fostered or adopted by parents of another race, it appeared frequently in discussions about Dolezal with rather different connotations, very much inflected by the sense of "trans" used in discussing Caitlyn Jenner. If one could have female subjectivity yet be born in a male body, many wondered, couldn't one also have black subjectivity in a white body? What, then, would it mean to speak of black/white or male/female subjectivity?

What such questions, and the discussions around them, often missed is that while race and gender identity intersect, the discourses around them do not function in exactly the same way. For instance, we might also ask: why did a wealthy and powerful white celebrity like Jenner generate visibility and acceptance for trans-women in a way that, say, black transgender actress Laverne Cox of the critically acclaimed television series *Orange is the New Black* did not? What does accepting and affirming Caitlyn Jenner's identity, or even marching in a hoodie in solidarity with Trayvon Martin, mean when transgender people, particularly trans people of color, are being simultaneously marginalized, brutalized, and victimized across the country while scarcely garnering any attention at all?[4] Why does a white woman passing as black generate discussions about racialization and identity in a way that a long history of African American "passing" has not, and how is passing as white different from passing as black?

Carla Kaplan (2015) takes up this last question, noting that so-called "voluntary Negroes"—individuals such as former NAACP head Walter Francis White, who refused to pass as white despite having pale skin, light hair, and blue eyes—were celebrated for expressing their loyalty to fellow African Americans by renouncing the potential privileges of claiming whiteness. Yet, Kaplan also points out that critiques of passing and calls for black loyalty and solidarity also "risked supporting the pernicious notion that race was innate, biological, predetermined, or fixed—the ideology that we call 'essentialism'" (Kaplan 2015). Thus, so called voluntary Negroes like White had to walk a thin line to "avoid shoring up everything they opposed" (Kaplan 2015). Kaplan juxtaposes this history against a surprisingly long history of whites, particularly women, who, perhaps inspired by these voluntary Negroes, wanted to volunteer themselves for blackness during the early twentieth century. Many of them, much like Dolezal, expressed that they felt "isolated and alienated" among fellow whites and desired to pass as black either out of "empathy and solidarity" for African Americans, or as a way to claim the inherent mutability and flexibility—"fluidity"—of racial identity. In light of our discussion of black fashion subjectivity above, this seems to beg the uncomfortable question of whether these women's attempts to construct transracial identities should also be considered examples of a push for more ontological possibilities over against circumscriptions of their identity. Should Dolezal's hair braids and headwraps be considered analogous to Martin's hoodie, in terms of how both express their subjectivity through an embodiment of style? Is it possible to argue otherwise without also asserting that race is in some way an inherent or fixed trait?

This is where Fanon's distinction between the "racial epidermal schema" and the underlying historical narrative of race is particularly helpful, as it exposes the "fluidity" and transposability of racial identity as characteristics of the performance of whiteness rather than of race as such. This is not because blackness is fixed in and by itself, but because it is fixed via a structuring narrative of white supremacy. Blackness is fixed so that whiteness can be "fluid" at the same time that this very connection is disavowed. Accepting Dolezal's defense for her passing as black requires us to privilege her subjectivity and perspective over against those of the black community and society as a whole—a privilege which is itself a mark of whiteness and its disproportionate access to a multitude of subject positions that do not inherently risk social stigmatization and/

or violent victimization. This is not an essential, innate, or fixed trait of white-skinned people, but rather a product of the structuring narrative of race itself. Subjectivity, as we have seen, is not simply a matter of individual self-expression, but rather exists in the entanglements between individuals and society through the strands of power relations, social norms, and the disciplinary and regulatory mechanisms of the state. So long as society continues to shore up its own construction of race in essentialist, ontological terms, claims such as Dolezal's will have no purchase. In this sense, however much we might applaud Kaplan in pointing out the falsity or "illogic" of this construction of race, the effects of being identified (as opposed to identifying) as black are indeed concrete rather than illusory; and as we saw with Trayvon Martin, they can even be fatal. When we set Dolezal's story in relief against Martin's, this difference is manifest even at the level of the grammar itself, as black is something Martin was *identified* as, with all of its problematic associations (passive voice, fixed in place by an external gaze with criminality read onto the body from the outside), whereas we speak in this instance of Dolezal's *identifying* (active, voluntary expression of agency and subjectivity) as black.

In keeping with this, Dolezal's "blackness" came with an opt-out clause that is simply not available for Martin. If things did not work out or if she simply changed her mind, she could at any time change her clothes, straighten her hair, and go back to being white. As Jelani Cobb (2015) argues, everyone is in some way clothed "in a fictive garb of race whose determinations are as arbitrary as they are damaging", but Dolezal's fluid transracial identity is particularly problematic in that her blackness is "as impermanent as burnt cork [and its] profitability rests upon an unspoken suggestion that the surest evidence of white superiority is the capacity to exceed blacks even at being black" (Cobb 2015). Dolezal's offense consisted not so much in her transgressing an absolute color line as in the fact that she knew the troubling history of institutionalized rape that has produced so many light (and even white) shades of blackness, and yet was still willing to take advantage of this history so that African Americans would take her at her word about her racial identity.

Cobb's analysis is helpful in that he holds in tension the concerns about racial essentialism and its social construction. While he firmly declares that Dolezal is not black, Cobb nevertheless finds her dishonesty less problematic than much of the language and assumptions being used to criticize her:

If blackness is simply a matter of a preponderance of African ancestry, then we should set about the task of excising a great deal of the canon of black history, up to and including the current President [Barack Obama]. If it is simply a matter of shared experience, we might excommunicate people like Walter White, whose blue eyes were camouflage that could serve both to spare him the direct indignity of racism and enable him to personally investigate and expose lynchings [...] Our means of defining ourselves are complex and contradictory—and could be nothing other than that. But if the rubric is faulty it remains vital [...] for black people, that past remains at the surface—close at hand, indelible, a narrative as legible as skin. (Cobb 2015)

In sum, race may indeed be a lie, but it is also a "fictive garb" that clothes real bodies in ways that affect and structure the very narratives they are "read" into, placing lethal (and legal) limits on the subject positions available to those whose darker hues of skin inflect their bodies with meanings they never created and certainly never chose. But does that foreclose the possibility of a transracial identity altogether?

COMPLEX TRANS-SUBJECTIVITY?

In "When I Was White", Sarah Valentine seizes the public furor over Dolezal to tell her own story about transracial identity (Valentine 2015). Biracial by birth, Valentine was raised by her biological mother and her mother's husband, who Valentine was led to assume (incorrectly) was her biological father. The family seldom discussed race and her parents deflected other people's confused questions about their daughter's ethnicity by referring to her as "olive" by virtue of a partial Italian ancestry. She recalls how, as a teenager, her mother would confiscate her hip-hop albums, Rasta hats, basketball jerseys, and "anything that smacked of African-America" from her room without giving a reason (Valentine 2013). Her high school friends used to joke that the school's ethnic demographics changed depending on how she wore her hair on a given day (ibid.). While others outside her family clearly already saw her as black, at home this was always explained away. Several years after leaving home for college and graduate school, she received a phone call from her mother, confessing that her biological father had indeed been a black man. Valentine asks, "If I am mixed race and black, what do I do with the white sense of self I lived with for 27 years, and how does one become black?" (Valentine 2015).

Here is a case that shows the identity entanglements of individual and society from the other side. In this case, it is (white) society that has already "read" her as black, while her own subjectivity and cultural upbringing had restricted her capacity to fully realize or express this. Her subsequent process of transracial identification became a ruptural event within her subjectivity as well as in her familial and social relationships. Her struggle for complex subjectivity played out physically on her body through the numerous physical and emotional maladies she went through in the process, effects of her coming to terms with the particular physicality of her (black) body. This was made even more difficult for her because family members did not understand why it was such a crisis for her. She was raised to believe in a purportedly "colorblind" ideology which nevertheless tacitly maintained that race was something only people of color had: "In my white family and white community, race was a problem for other people, but not for us [...] And, despite discredited notions of biological essentialism, it was assumed to be an intrinsic quality" (Valentine 2015).

Perhaps what is most striking about the way Valentine frames her attempt to navigate her transracial identity is how it resembles what Pinn has identified as the impulse for complex subjectivity. One of the key ways in which this manifests is through the triadic structure of conversion narratives as marked by a painful existential encounter with historic identity, a struggle for renewal from the previous mode of consciousness, and finally an embracing of a new consciousness and new modes of behavior in community (Pinn 2003, 158–9).

Valentine uses similar terms when she describes how it took her years of "painful reckoning to shed that [old, white] psychology and create a new one that allowed her to see and love her own blackness and to forgive the little white girl who did not know any better" (Valentine 2015). In contrast to conversion narratives within established faith traditions, however, Valentine uses words like "psychology" rather than spirituality in order to tell her story of reconciling herself; she is being reconciled not to a divine or spiritual reality but to her own black body. Like many runaway slaves and black radicals such as Malcolm X, she chose to mark this conversion by formally changing her name. Her reason was that, "I needed to make a definitive break with the person I had been, with the person my family had told me I was. I no longer wanted to be complicit in the lie of whiteness; I needed to define my identity on my own terms" (ibid.). She finally had an answer to the ontologically troubling question "What are you?" that her body seemed to automatically elicit from (white) others. Her answer is one that holds multiple ontological possibilities in tension and that challenges binary assumptions about identity and subjectivity. Despite her ongoing struggle to comprehend and express her identity, and despite being initially bewildered by not knowing exactly "how to be black", she says that in time, "I came out of it with a cohesive sense of self that embodies all its contradictions" (ibid.).

Valentine's self-fashioning embodies what Pinn describes as "a push or desire for 'fullness'" and a "healthy self-concept" that is borne out of a response to an existential crisis of identity and meaning (Pinn 2003, 173). Her journey also evokes, albeit in a slightly different sense, Kaiser and McCullough's conception of fashion subjectivity as entailing knotted nodes of meaning that are processually made and unmade, revealing the entanglements of race, dress, and the body (Kaiser and McCullough 2010). After discovering her racial identity, she became constantly aware of the fact that she was now not only "wearing" blackness but that before, without ever thinking explicitly about it, she had been "wearing" whiteness. This change of consciousness echoes the sense in which black fashion subjectivity is often less about *what* is worn than *how* it is worn. To that end, Valentine ponders whether there are "certain black ways" of doing things, or if her behavior will now begin to change to reflect her "official blackness" (Valentine 2013). She becomes aware that the "how" of black fashion subjectivity does not stem from intrinsic racial traits, but rather from a shared consciousness of embodiment: "African Americans are not allowed to forget that they are walking around, picking out groceries, driving their kids to school while being black" (ibid.). What is striking about Valentine's account is that she chooses not to describe her new racial consciousness in terms of the ways that social norms attempt to push against and restrict expressions of black subjectivity and the consequences this might entail for her. Instead, her narrative shifts from the denial and confusion of her upbringing to an eager embrace of her new identity as she takes pleasure in the aesthetic beauty of her blackness, which she can now wear without shame or confusion, and in the ways in which being able to name her blackness opens up the possibility of working out the interweaving facets of her experience in community with others who share her struggle.

(AD)DRESSING BLACK RELIGION

We have seen how readings of bodies "dressed" by markers of race, gender, and sexuality, and the narratives that structure their interpretation, can be deeply problematic, damaging, and even deadly. Yet, we have also seen that the kind of aesthetic shift created by new narratives of body and self, by new compartments of style and movement in the world, can constitute important sites for the production of religious meaning in the mundane. That is to say, as a site for creating, expressing, or perceiving meaning, everyday dress can be understood as a religious phenomenon without necessitating explicit connections to either religious institutions with their associated norms of dress or fashion design as an explicit mode of cultural production.

Reflecting on the intersections between race, religion, and dress, Robert Beckford (2009) cautions against the tendency to always reduce forms of black creative expression to some form of instrumentality—whether religious, social, or political. In terms reminiscent of our discussion of black independent film in Chapter 5, Beckford suggests that the aesthetic quality of expression, in this case through dress, is valuable in itself as it "signals elements of delight, the erotic and pleasurable". Everyday fashion need not always be read as an "act of rebellion but also as an act of pleasure, to capture the 'cool' of the 'world'" (pp. 145-9).

Indeed, inquiry into this "in itself" aspect of aesthetics is what Pinn calls for in his introductory chapter to *Black Religion and Aesthetics* (the same volume that contains Beckford's essay). Pinn argues that there is an "aesthetic shift" within black religion which counters the representational logic of white superiority so that, "the once despised Black body is rendered, at least in momentary spurts, valuable". This is a central aspect of black religion and its performance on and through the body (Pinn 2009, 7-8). While Pinn's analysis has focused mainly on aspects of cultural production, our focus on everyday dress as it connects to the ways in which bodies are always "dressed" by various markers of identity allows us to locate aspects of this "aesthetic shift" onto the body itself. That is to say, dressing practices become an important way of presenting black bodies as valued and beautiful over against normative discourses that attempt to restrict or deny expressions of black humanity. At the same time, however, the aesthetic shift effected by dress should not be conceived exclusively as an intentional response (political or otherwise) to oppressive forces from the outside. In an everyday context, dress is best thought of as another aspect of "just being", in the sense we discussed in Chapter 5. Just being and feeling beautiful in the way one presents and dresses the body is already an example of the kinds of counter-discourse that are integral to expressions of black religion.

This discussion helps us to better articulate the theory of black religion as it relates to embodiment and the quest for complex subjectivity. This is not simply because dress gives us an example that is visually and aesthetically stimulating, that cannot itself be adequately described apart from the body, and that is universally relatable as an aspect of everyday practice. As we have seen, dress is also deeply connected to individual, cultural, religious, and political constructions of meaning; it both shapes and is shaped by our discursive embodied identity, even as it adorns, equips, and facilitates the way our material bodies move in and through the(ir) world(s). Style is both an action and a statement, whether implicit (through unconscious compliance with dress codes or internalized norms in tacit support and acquiescence), or explicit (through deliberate rebellion against or deviation from those norms and codes). Yet, there is no single grammar, semiotics, or hermeneutic key with which we can read or interpret the meaning of dress and the dressed body. Instead there is a constellation of various intersectional factors—race, class, (trans/cis)gender, nationality, and so on—that coalesce in time and space with particular clothes, bodies, narratives, and actions, before any interpretation takes place.

The stories of Martin, Dolezal, and Valentine reveal how contentious and fraught issues of race and identity truly are. But what these stories also tell us is that in addition to the phenomenal experience of individual bodies, the practices of reading and interpreting (and judging and reacting to) the "dressed" black body also matter a great deal. Fanon says, "under white eyes, the only real eyes. I am fixed [...] they objectively cut away slices of my reality", all the while weaving together a replacement reality, his "uniform" (Fanon 1967, 116). For Rachel Dolezal, whiteness can be a coat of many colors that can, with braids, headwraps, self-tanning, and a post at the NAACP, even don this dark "uniform" for a while. For Trayvon Martin, the combination of dark skin and a hoodie wove together to form a veil that prevented and in some ways still prevents his humanity from being seen by others. For Sarah Valentine, awareness of her blackness was an awakening into an aesthetic embrace of new and expanding ontological possibilities. What is perhaps most striking about this study of dress is that we can have such complex and nuanced conversation—the implications of which have the power to shape and even take lives—around something so simple and banal as a hooded sweatshirt and a headwrap. *What* we wear every day, from the clothes we put on to the markers of identity that already "dress" our bodies, is a rich tapestry of interwoven meanings; *how* we wear them can tell us a great deal about the ways in which identities become fixed, and more expansive possibilities for subjectivity are struggled for, upon the very surface of the body itself.

NOTES

1. For clarity, whenever they refer to this wider, or metaphorical, sense of being "dressed" or "clothed" in a "garment" of race/gender/sexuality, such words will appear in quotes. When written without quotes they refer to dressing, clothing and garments in the ordinary sense of textiles, fabrics, etc.
2. For a theological analysis of Trayvon Martin's life and death, see Douglas (2015). Douglas calls for a shift in focus away from the problematics of redemptive suffering in both Jesus' and Martin's "crucifying death" toward a focus on the hopeful possibilities of resurrection. Martin's resurrection is accomplished by his parents, friends and other family members telling the full story of his life as a move away from the domineering shadow cast over it by his death.
3. For an extensive critique of the differences entailed by transracial and transgender identities see Heyes (2006).
4. See for example Samantha Michaels, "It's Incredibly Scary to Be a Transgender Woman of Color Right Now," *Mother Jones*, June 26, 2015, accessed on August 15, 2015, http://www.motherjones.com/politics/2015/06/transgender-women-disproportionately-targeted-violent-hate-crimes; Terrell Jermaine Starr, "Violence Against Black Transgender Women Goes Largely Ignored," *The Root*, January 23, 2015, accessed on August 15, 2015, http://www.theroot.com/articles/culture/2015/01/violence_against_black_transgender_women_goes_largely_ignored.html

Chapter Eight

Gathering around the Table: Food Practices and Religious Meaning

Perhaps no activity contributes to our understanding of social relationships, cultural identity, and religious community more than our rituals surrounding food preparation and consumption. In the social context, we rarely ever share meals with strangers. We gather around the table to eat with family, friends, and business associates. These gatherings are often the times when we share the events of our lives with one another, catch up on old times, and solidify relationships. Whether we are celebrating a wedding or commemorating a significant accomplishment, such as graduation, we often gather around the table and consume food.

Food contributes to our sense of cultural identity. It is, for instance, hard to imagine major holidays such as Thanksgiving and Independence Day without thinking of traditional foods that go with them such as turkey, barbeque, potato salad, or baked beans. Food codes and food rituals are often essential to expressions of religious piety and the initiation into particular religious communities. Food rituals serve simultaneously as religious symbols, as the subject or prayer, as a marker of communion, and as a distinct marker of inclusion and exclusion (Anderson 2005, 154). Whether it is through the ritual practices of occasional fasting or through weekly rituals of sharing a common meal, food helps to solidify communities. Through food, people share common bonds, shared realities, and display commitments to religious and social ideals. In sum, our food is a form of religious expression.

However, this link between food and religion is not always understood in a positive way. In his autobiographical novel, *Black Boy* (1946), Richard Wright writes, for instance, that he became disillusioned with institutionalized religion when he was faced with the very real biochemical responses of his body to the condition of hunger. As a practicing Seventh-day

Adventist, Wright's family posed restrictions on available food options, even in instances of extreme hunger and poverty. For instance, although readily available in his community, pork and catfish were forbidden. Wright blamed his hunger, partly, on these religious food restrictions. Because he would not accept the teachings of the Seventh-day Adventists over his need to satisfy his bodily needs, Wright became an outcast in his own home.

While this is one example of the intersections of food practices and religion, we will approach the relationship between food and religion in a slightly different way. If religion can be understood as the quest for complex subjectivity, then the ways in which we consume, prepare, and think about food in our daily lives could be understood as religious. Whether one wants to follow the Atkins diet and cut carbohydrates, or eat foods unaltered by human science or technology such as proponents of the Paleo diet, food practices seem to speak to the existential and ontological questions of life and, in doing so, take on religious quality.

In this chapter, we will discuss in particular the religious nature of black veganism. We will explore how this diet helps African Americans create meaning through what they put into their bodies. The old adage that we are what we eat is true in the sense that what we eat contributes to our identities and sense of self. Veganism is a way of life that seeks to exclude all forms of exploitation of and cruelty toward animals, and therefore refrains from using animals for food consumption, clothing, other consumable goods, or product testing. While vegans have complex and varying sets of beliefs and practices surrounding this abstinence, most include an interest in environmental sustainability and social justice in the production of food. Typically, they also prefer organic and minimally processed foods that have not been genetically modified (non-GMOs) by the application of scientific technology to agriculture. In sum, veganism can be understood as not only a way of eating, but also a way of life (Phillips 2009, 9). Those who commit to the vegan way of life do so for various reasons including ethics, health concerns, political commitments, and philosophical or spiritual beliefs (ibid.).

CAPITALISM AND ITS DISCONTENTS

Many vegans take issue with the contamination and destruction of nature. Since nature is of the utmost importance for black vegans, specifically those who become vegans for ethical reasons, anything that tampers with or violates nature, its creatures, or its resources is vehemently opposed. Such practices have been intensified by capitalism, which results in the exploitation of natural resources and human labor out of the pursuit of profit. Such is evidenced, for instance, in the treatment of animals. Some argue that the systematic (ab)use of animals for capital and food is conceptually related to the system that allowed for humans to be herded and enslaved in the United States—a system that classified certain human beings as chattel, along with other non-human animals. The (ab)use of enslaved Africans and non-human animals in capitalism began with the herding of animals. The commodification of non-human animals for food production and their use as beasts of burden could be considered one of the precursors for the enslavement, oppression, and slaughter of human beings (Tuttle 2004, 18–19). There is a deep connection here. In fact, the word "capital" is derived from the Latin word *capita*, which means "head", as in a head of cattle or sheep. Sheep, cattle, goats, and other livestock were the first forms of capital.

The way that animals are treated in factory farms is but one example of how capitalism and herding culture can contaminate and destroy nature. Most chickens in factory farms are, for instance, not allowed to roam freely and walk through grass, breathe fresh air, or enjoy fresh water (Drew 2009, 62). In addition to food consumption, humans exploit non-human animals for milk, eggs, fur, and other products. Capitalism has also changed the way humans view their relationship to nature; initially, human beings viewed themselves as a part of nature. Since capitalism has spread across the globe, human beings have sought ever-increasing ways of harnessing and controlling nature for their own ends. The domination of non-human animals and land has caused countless conflicts with other humans over land. The land is necessary in order to allow the herd to graze. As constant grazing obliterates the vegetation, herders are forced to seek more land, which they will take by any means.

In addition, many vegans have concerns about the restrictions imposed on the movement of animals. They also argue that the use of land for grazing is inefficient and actually contributes to the destruction of ecosystems. The vast amounts of land required for feeding livestock, they contend, would be better served by producing fruits and vegetables, rotating the crops so that these can continue to supply the land with nutrients. To be sure, if it takes an acre of land to adequately feed one cow that will eventually be processed as steak, that same acre of land, if it were used to produce fruits and vegetables, would be able to produce up to five times the nutritional value than the cattle can provide while also maintaining the integrity of the ecosystem (Belasco 2006, 57).

Moreover, vegans worry that the consumption of meat could possibly transfers toxins from the animal to the body of the person who eats it. For African Americans, all but one of the leading causes of death (accidents) has a connection to diet and lifestyle. For instance, more than 75 percent of African Americans are overweight or obese.[1] Obesity, in turn, has a strong correlation to diabetes. Many vegans consider an all plant or nearly plant diet to be one of the most effective ways to stop the progression of heart disease, reversing the tendency to obesity, and controlling the onset of diabetes (Loyd-Page 2009, 6).

Certain aspects of capitalist production lend themselves to contaminating the food supply due to the chemicals that are used to boost the production of food and make it more cost-efficient. The desire to make food products that are quick and easy to prepare has led to the creation of "food-like" substances, products that are marketed as food but have been stripped of most or all of their nutritional value and, in some cases, may even cause harm to bodies. We find such "plastic" foods both at home and at fast food restaurants. After World War II, food processing changed from mechanically breaking down crops such as wheat and oats for the purpose of packaging, to applying chemicals to create new foods such as Tang, margarine, instant pudding, instant oatmeal, and turkey bacon (Belasco 2006, 37). In addition, manufacturers began to use chemicals to bleach food to reduce the decay and rotting of food and increase profits for the manufacturer. Flour and sugar, for instance, naturally brown, were stripped of all color and treated with preservatives in order to increase shelf life (Belasco 2006, 50).

SOUL FOOD AND ITS DISCONTENTS

Black veganism could also be understood as a response to another cultural food tradition: soul food. Soul food includes animal products—usually discarded parts of the animal such as neckbones, hog maws, pork chops, fatback, porgies—as well as non-animal foods like turnips, pot liquor, kale, watermelon, black-eyed peas, grits, gravy, hushpuppies, hoecake, buttermilk biscuits, pancakes, dumplings, and more (Witt 2004, 82). Deep-fried meats, oftentimes smothered in cream-based gravies, are prevalent. Vegetables are slow-cooked with pork and in pork fat, and desserts are loaded with butter and cream. As a result, soul food is often said to be a "heart-attack on a plate" (Loyd-Page 2009, 6).

Although soul food has been an important part of the creation and consolidation of black identity and black culture within a context of suffering and oppression (Gregory 1974, 78), it is also related to the history of chattel slavery, the commodification of black bodies and the exploitation of their labor. Believed to be the diet that African Americans consumed during slavery, it has its roots in the rural South. Soul food became popular in the 1960s, after World War II and during the Civil Rights movement. According to Witt, the term soul has two meanings. It refers, first, to the seemingly indefinable and unverifiable part of the body that has been conventionally understood in numerous faith traditions as distinguishing humans from other animals in the natural world. Second, the term soul can refer to a genre of music in and of itself, as well as the emotional and improvisational way of making music that has been associated with other African American genres such as jazz and blues (Witt 2004, 80).

Although an important part of black culture, soul food has also been controversial as an increasing number of African Americans are rejecting the cuisine due to its associations with slavery and poor health. Consider, for instance, the food codes of the Nation of Islam (NOI), articulated by Elijah Muhammad, which are used, in ways similar to black veganism, to reclassify black bodies in the midst of an oppressive society. We already noted in Chapter 2 that Clarence 13X, founder of the Five Percenters, followed Muhammad's food codes and urged his followers to do the same. Muhammad claimed that consuming the same food products as the enslaved Africans once did constitutes participation in the legacy of chattel slavery and a denial of one's true identity. Muhammad maintained that, during slavery, African Americans in the twentieth century were still left with the unwanted and undesirable scraps of animal organs, despite the fact that the country had been blessed by Allah with plenty of good food and water.

The food that enslaved Africans were fed reinforced their "animal" status in the eyes of the slave owners: enslaved Africans often labored on a diet of nothing more than cornmeal, white bread, and tainted pork and fish. The portion sizes were inadequate, which resulted in frequent malnourishment. Some slaves attempted to avoid starvation by following the slave master's children in order to collect the crumbs. According to Hopkins, enslaved people were treated like "pig litters" (Hopkins 1999, 73–4). Katie Cannon corroborates the argument that African Americans were described as and treated like animals: they were corralled, transported, and auctioned off like livestock, whilst being referred to as "stock", "brood sows", and "breeders", to name just a few (Cannon 1998, 29). Furthermore, when an enslaved African died, insurance companies would compensate the owner for their loss of *chattel*. Bondspersons were routinely listed as assets alongside other "property" such as the farm equipment and livestock on loan applications (Hopkins 1999, 54–5). In redefining black bodies, black vegans seek to challenge these objectifying classifications.

HER NAME IS MOTHER NATURE

Black vegans consider black people to be responsible for protecting humans, non-human animals, and nature from over-exploitation. As such, respect and reliance upon nature is considered to be an important factor in the restoration of society's relationship with nature. And although there are black vegans that may participate in varying degrees in institutionalized religious traditions or maintain theistic beliefs, nature is nevertheless often accorded special status as a holy, transcendent other (Gregory 1974, 5–7). For vegans, nature contains all that we need to live a long and sustainable life. They reason that if human beings would use natural food products and natural medicine, they would not suffer from as many diseases, mental health problems, or succumb to premature death (Ifateyo 2009, 112).

Ajowa Ifateyo suggests that "Mother Nature" has created human beings as her most intelligent animals, and humans are therefore considered to be ultimately responsible for the care of nature's other plants and creatures. Accordingly, non-human animals hold a special place in the eyes of vegans and require special attention. Similar to humans, non-human animals have a central nervous system, which enables them to move through the world and causes them to feel pain. They have some level of consciousness. When human beings consume other animals for food, we inflict undue suffering on these animals. Moreover, while we feast on the flesh, muscles and internal organs of animals after we kill them, we have become sanitized to this fact, because the nature of our society has distanced the average person from the bloodletting that is necessary in order for us to eat meat.

Vegan activist and comedian Dick Gregory connects the killing and consumption of animal flesh to the larger non-violent movement in the 1960s. He states:

> I became totally committed to nonviolence, and I was convinced that nonviolence meant opposition to killing in any form. I felt the commandment "Thou shalt not kill" applied to human beings not only in their dealings with

each other—war, lynching, assassination, murder and the like—but in their practice of killing animals for food or sport. Animals and humans suffer and die alike. Violence causes the same pain, the same spilling of blood, the same stench of death, the same arrogant, cruel and brutal taking of life. (Gregory 1974, 15–16)

Gregory became convinced that the killing of animals for food is immoral and against nature. He writes, "I refused to accept that I had to stoop to the lowliness of killing something to get my dinner" (Gregory 1974, 16).

Some vegans believe that unlike eating animal flesh, consuming plants does not cause any pain and suffering. In fact, we are often not even eating the plant itself. When we eat plant-based food, we usually eat the fruit or the seeds that have been released from grasses, herbs, trees, vines, and other plants. The plant is often left alive and able to continue to produce for seed and fruit. For example, grains such as wheat, oats, and corn are actually seeds and fruits of cereal grasses. Legumes such as lentils, peas, and beans are the seed of leguminous plants. Fruit and berries, such as apples and blueberries, are released from trees and vines. Consuming these foods does not destroy the plant that produces them. The tree or the vine continues to live, producing fruit. The only exception is when we eat roots and seed-bearing flowers such as carrots and broccoli, respectively (Tuttle 2004, 7).

BLACK VEGAN RELIGIOUS ETHICS

Black vegans are concerned with three areas in their ethical worldview: nature, health, and life. As a worldview, veganism could function as a form of highly individualized religion within the context of a community, even including a system of ethics that guides vegans in how they should act in the world (Dyczewska 2008). Black vegans are often concerned with both the content of their food and the conditions in which the food, and other products they consume, are produced, including their ecological impact. This extends beyond the consumption of food, as black vegans are concerned about the standard of living they create for all animals and humans that participate in the process of manufacturing, selling, burying, and disposing animal products (Santosa 2009, 75).

As part of a community that is often stricken with ailments and diseases such as high cholesterol, obesity, and other forms of suffering, black vegans are intentional about living a life in optimum health, protecting the ecosystem, and preventing the undue suffering of other animals (Drew 2009,

63). African Americans who are attentive to the pain and suffering that other animals experience, realize that they are emotionally connected to other beings. Moreover, Meadows has argued that when we see animals suffering in poor conditions, we should think of the more than two million Americans who are confined within the prison-industrial complex, or economically disadvantaged workers who face poor labor conditions in the food industry (2009, 151).

As we noted above, American society obscures the source of our food through capitalistic production. Unless one is a hunter or fisherman, very few people in our society are involved with the capture, killing, and butchering of their own food, especially meat. It is common for us to go to a grocery store or market and find our meat pre-butchered, prepared, and pre-packaged for us, completely desensitizing us to the reality that we are about to consume an animal that once breathed, moved, and walked the earth. We did not peer into its eyes as it took its last breath, we did not see, feel, or smell the blood that it lost, or feel its body as we cut into it and removed its organs. As noted, veganism's concerns are not limited to the food that we eat, but extend to any products where animals have been used in the manufacturing or testing. Black vegans tend to support products that are organic, made from natural plants, unencumbered by pesticides and chemicals. This includes clothing, and hygiene products such as soap, shampoo, toothpaste, and deodorant.

Black veganism, then, can be seen as a religious act that helps us to understand who, what and where we are in an oppressive world dominated by capitalism and white supremacy and with a legacy of herding and dominating nature. As black vegans come to understand their connection to nature and position in an oppressive society, they abstain from consuming meat and inflicting the same harm on their fellow creatures (Gregory 1974, 20). Although black veganism may not fit into more traditional definitions of religion, veganism helps African Americans navigate the world and respond to the various forms of oppression they experience.

NOTES

1 See "Obesity Prevention in Black Communities", September 2014. Available from: stateofobesity.org/disparities/blacks (accessed March 2, 2017).

Chapter Nine

Every-Body's Truth: The New Genetics of Race and the Quest for Complex Subjectivity

Biological understandings of race have historically been used as a racist weapon against African Americans. In the nineteenth and twentieth centuries, modern scientific theories of race as a biological feature of the human body legitimated and enforced the order of white supremacy by classifying the bodies of African Americans as biologically distinct from and inferior to white European bodies. In the second half of the twentieth century, essentialist biological classifications of race were discredited and largely purged from mainstream public discourse. However, with the mapping of the human genome at the turn of the twenty-first century, biological classifications of race reemerged within the biological sciences, most notably in the field of genetics. While genetic understandings of race are still being used to precarious ends within the medical and political spheres, many people are finding significant life meaning in the ability to connect genetic bodily material to historical and cultural genealogies and narratives. Especially in the burgeoning industry of "ancestor tracing", where genetic bodily material is extracted in order to connect bodies to historical and geographical communities, these connections mark the body's most basic, mundane material as a site for the quest for complex subjectivity. Following chapters that addressed the ways that bodies are adorned, and what food they (refuse to) consume, "Every-body's Truth", which explores the body itself as the ultimate site of the mundane, will conclude our exploration of the nexus between body and religion—in everyday forms of religion, as well as for *Embodiment and Black Religion* more generally.

BIOLOGICAL RACE IN THE NINETEENTH AND EARLY TWENTIETH CENTURIES

As part of a radical conceptual shift in scientific knowledge with the publication of Charles Darwin's *Origin of the Species* in 1859, modern western ideas of race were inserted into nineteenth-century biological taxonomies of human difference. Though biology had been a factor in previous constructions of race,[1] in the second half of the nineteenth century it became the central category for understanding racial differences across the human species. With significant advances in the biological, zoological, botanical, and geological sciences, the scientific paradigm of knowledge that privileged empirical verification and deductive classification gradually eclipsed older paradigms of religious and folk beliefs about race. In its modern biological frame, a body has a race in the same sense that a body has a sex. However, unlike biological sex, which (according to nineteenth-century racial science) divides the human species into two distinct biological categories that span across other markers of difference such as hair or skin color, race was considered to be a biological classification that divides the human species into *multiple* typological subgroups with distinct physical, intellectual, and behavioral characteristics. In "On the Natural Variety of Mankind" (Blumenbach [1975] 1999), nineteenth-century physiologist Johann Friedrich Blumenbach famously divided the human species into five groups, each with its own distinct characteristics: Caucasian, Mongolian, Ethiopian, American, and Malay. Each group had its own distinct bodily and intellectual markers. Consider, for instance, this fragment of Blumenbach's description of the Caucasian race: "colour white, cheeks rosy...hair brown or chestnut coloured...head subglobular...face oval, straight, its parts moderately defined, forehead smooth, nose narrow, slightly hooked, mouth small" (p. 201). Comparatively, he describes the Ethiopian race as having "colour black...hair black and curly...head narrow, compressed at the sides...forehead knotty...uneven, malar bones protruding outward; eyes very prominent; nose thick, mixed up as it were with the wide jaws" (p. 202).

While nineteenth-century science focused on the body's external traits such as head size and skin color, with the turn of the twentieth century, biological understandings of race turned inward. Emerging with Gregor Mendel's theories of gene inheritance in the late nineteenth century, the burgeoning field of genetics made it possible to conceive race as a genetic distinction that goes well beyond the outer appearance of a body. Genetics is especially interested in the idea of heredity, or the passing of biological traits from one organism to another through sexual reproduction. The theory of heredity is particularly important for biological notions of race because it situates it as part of natural history and focuses on the variations of genetic transmissions of phenotype, behavior, and physicality across the human species. In the twentieth century, the theory of heredity became the primary explanation for why the human species is divided into separate races that display varying bodily and genetic features. In 1923, for example, the anthropologist Alfred Kroeber situated race within the basic process of procreation: "to the question why a Louisiana Negro is black and longheaded, the answer is ready. He was born so. As cows produce calves, and lions, cubs, so Negro springs from Negro and Caucasian from Caucasian. We call the force *heredity*" (Kroeber 1963, 2). Framed this way, race names a core part of human being's genetic makeup and therefore an irrefutable and permanent "truth" of the body and its relation to other bodies.

Of course, biological conceptions of race, including their genetic forms, are anything but neutral. The classifications "Negro" and "Caucasian" have never simply stood alone as, among other things, names for physical differences in phenotype. As long as biological conceptions of race have been employed, they have always functioned as a way to flatten out highly diverse geographical people groups—for example, "Africans" or "Europeans"—into monolithic "races" reduced to one-size-fits-all classifications of everything from cognitive capacity to social behavior. In this way, it is easy to understand how framing race as a biological reality serves ideological purposes. In the late nineteenth and twentieth centuries, white Americans justified a Jim Crow society through appeals to African American's supposed cognitive inferiority and their particular labor capacities, both seen as biological conditions (Washington 2008, 143–56; Roberts 2011b, 1–26). The "African race" as a whole was seen as cognitively inferior and suited for hard physical labor because their biological makeup supposedly conditioned their bodies as such. As Charles Davenport, an important figure in the American eugenics movement, argued, "there is a constitutional, hereditary, genetic basis for the difference between [whites and blacks] in mental tests. We have to conclude that there are racial differences in mental capacity" (Davenport 1928). Genetic knowledge solidified the racial hierarchy of white supremacy as an unalterable biological reality written into nature. The inferior mental capacity of Africans, it was argued, could not be improved by education or a change in environment. Because it was thought to be a permanent fixture of biological reality, racial status could not be transcended. The mixing of black and white bodies was therefore seen as biologically dangerous. Miscegenation was understood to be counter to nature's proper order. Interracial sex could produce offspring that would dilute the "purity" of the white gene pool and therefore challenge the clearly demarcated racial lines that separate whites from other races.

CONTEMPORARY BIOLOGICAL RACE

In the second half of the twentieth century biological understandings of race largely dropped out of fashion, at least in the academic mainstream of the sciences and humanities. In response to the Holocaust and other horrific programs of racial and ethnic cleansing, scientific advances in genomic knowledge, and decolonization and civil rights movements across the globe, race as a biological category was discredited as dangerous and increasingly seen as a bogus scientific category. In 1963, for example, the United Nations issued a statement strongly condemning biological understandings of racial hierarchy as having no place in human discourse, stating that "any doctrine of racial differentiation or superiority is scientifically false, morally condemnable, socially unjust and dangerous, and that there is no justification for racial discrimination either in theory or in practice" (United Nations General Assembly 1963). That biological racial categories dropped out of fashion did not mean that racism stopped or even subsided, but rather that appeals to biological difference as a basis for assigning superiority or inferiority largely became socially and politically taboo. As many scholars have argued, racism is now practiced primarily along the lines of culture, not biology. Etienne Balibar speaks of this in terms of a "neo-racism", "whose dominant theme is not biological heredity but the insurmountability of cultural differences, a racism which, at first sight, does not postulate the superiority of certain groups or peoples in relation to others but 'only' the harmfulness of abolishing frontiers, the incompatibility of life-styles and traditions" (Balibar 1991, 21). This understanding of racism names a kind of "racism without race", where race has been evacuated of a biological essence that carries cognitive and behavioral predispositions (Bonilla-Silva 2009).

With these developments, it might seem that biological understandings of race have been relegated to the annals of history. However, in recent years there has been a resurging interest in race as a biological category in the genomic sciences that essentially thinks itself free of the kind of racist baggage that defined past eras. Despite the fact that in the last decade the Human Genome Project, which has successfully mapped the entire human genetic code, has proven that race is a fictive category that cannot be located within the genes of the human species, race continues to be interpreted as a legitimate biological category through which to analyze human difference (Roberts 2011a, x).

The reasons for the persistence of race as a biological category fall mostly within questions of genetic classification. As Dorothy Roberts notes, there is a new racial science that focuses on the 0.1 percent of human difference found across the human genetic code that, despite the genetic evidence that race cannot be reliably identified within genes, "is increasingly seen as encompassing race" (Roberts 2011a, 26). As Roberts describes, such a racial interpretation of the 0.1 percent of genetic difference is derived from old typologies of race that are applied, arbitrarily it seems, to genetic categories of racial difference:

> [T]he genetic variation found in the human species is not grouped in discrete, genetically distinct units scientists can identify as races. To the contrary, human genetic diversity occurs in a continuum that cannot be partitioned by clear boundaries and that crosses what are commonly considered racial lines. Consider how, in the United States, people with any amount of African ancestry are grouped together in one race. Yet the greatest amount of genetic diversity in the world exists in sub-Saharan Africa. (Roberts 2011a, 51)

Despite the complexity of human genetic diversity that makes any simple classificatory schema that divides the human species into distinct groups highly suspect, a significant number of scientists still claim that racial categories continue to have scientific validity. Many argue that the world's human population remains something that can be categorized according to old racial typographies including basic distinctions such as African, Asian, and Caucasian (Bliss 2012, 58). However neutrally these categories purport to function, race still functions as a mechanism that lumps diversely embodied individuals into predetermined categories of history and identity. In this way, contemporary medical knowledge of the human body at the genetic level maintains a link with older scientific discourses that situate the racial body within predetermined categories of meaning.

The persistence of old racial typologies shows that the resurgence of biological race within the genetic frame is not as objective as many of its advocates claim. The contemporary science of race, just like all science that preceded it, has its biases and blind spots. Because of this, biological notions of race still function as mechanisms of exclusion and objectification. For example, Roberts shows how biological racial profiling still occurs in medical institutions such as hospitals, often with open and enthusiastic support from scientists and doctors (Roberts 2011a, 81–103). The idea that race can provide more efficient and accurate means of diagnosis and profiling, however promising in terms of its application to individual cases, ends up creating major cracks into which racialized bodies, misdiagnosed or lumped into an ultimately irrelevant and unhelpful category, can fall through. For example, Roberts recalls the story of a female African American toddler with lung problems that was not given the test for cystic fibrosis, which is believed to be a genetic disorder not typical among African Americans (Roberts 2011a, 99). Because of her presumed biological "race", she was excluded from that particular medical consideration, and it took a long period of unnecessary suffering to notice that she actually had cystic fibrosis. Cases like this remain a common experience for African Americans, and are a continuation of the fraught historical relationship of African Americans and the medical establishment (Washington 2008).

There are also highly dubious legal and political consequences in the move to contemporary genetic understandings of race. Roberts outlines what she calls a "race-based biotechnology emerging from the genetic sciences" that reinforces social structures of systemic racism and criminalization (Roberts 2011a, 569). Laws passed over the last two decades in the US have led to the mass collection of genetic data from immigrant populations and those suspected or charged of crimes, often without their consent. For example, the Patriot Act of 2001 expanded the requirement of genetic collection from any terror related crime, while the DNA Fingerprint Act of 2005 authorizes law enforcement agents to collect and store DNA from anyone they arrest or detain (Roberts 2011b, 265–6). Such collections, unsurprisingly, function as a means for profiling racialized groups and contributing to communities of color becoming more and more vulnerable to state surveillance and suspicion.

RELIGION AND THE NEW GENETICS OF RACE

There is a general consensus within humanities and social science disciplines that race has no biological essence and that scientific claims to the contrary only further the racist legacy of biological race (Bliss 2012, 52). Yet, the new genetics of race has had a profound impact on how many people understand race, embodiment, and identity. While biological race generally produced negative images of African Americans as sub-human, contemporary understandings of race as a genetic category have become for many a mundane and positive source of life meaning. Genetic science has given many the sense that it really is possible to access and put to meaningful use the most basic and fundamental foundation of embodied nature. Knowledge of the human genome has opened up a conceptual space in which human beings connect their "natural" identities as embodied beings—which for many is still framed in terms of race—in ways that presumably transcend what are seen as social and political constructions of identity. Genetic knowledge supposedly reveals the body's truth, its unchangeable particularity separated from any social, political, or even outward physical imposition. A person can get plastic surgery to alter their outward appearance, signify another cultural identity through aesthetic markers such as clothing or hairstyle, or even feign, as discussed in Chapter 7, another race in the way Rachel Dolezal "lived" as an African American woman. Yet, a person cannot change their genetic makeup. When all is said and done, genomic notions of race and identity suggest that our genetic makeup holds the key to our "real" identity. For example, the self-identifying white supremacist Craig Cobb was invited on the talk show *The Trisha Goddard Show* to discuss his attempt to found an "all white" town in North Dakota and undergo a DNA diagnostics exam that would reveal his true racial "roots". Leading up to the unveiling of his genetic diagnosis, the show portrays Cobb as irrefutably "white", and his racism supposedly reinforces this fact beyond all doubts. Yet, his DNA analysis told a different story when it revealed that Cobb's DNA was comprised, as the diagnostics test described, of fourteen percent "Sub-Saharan African" genetic material.[2] As the African American host and other participants break into laughter at the revelation that, as the host tells him, "you have a little black in you", Cobb's identity suddenly takes on a whole new meaning. No matter how racially pure or "white" Cobb sees himself, deep down his "true" identity, according to how his DNA was classified, is fourteen percent racially black.

For many, the "truth" unlocked in DNA testing is not a negative experience of the inescapability of embodied particularity, as it was for Cobb, but rather a positive experience that unlocks an array of meaning and possibility. Genetic testing potentially opens up new ways to think about identity that connect bodies in meaningful ways to historical, cultural, and geographical sites of meaning beyond the present. In this way, knowledge of one's genetic makeup and its application to the construction of meaning can be considered part of one's quest for complex subjectivity. A good example of this is how genetic material is interpreted as a link to ancestry. The spectacle of Cobb's "Sub-Saharan African" identity on the talk show is part of a growing interest in tracing ancestry for people who wish to attain knowledge of their "roots". Where one comes from, family history, connection to historical events, places, and people: all these things are claimed as extractable from one's genetic makeup.

For some African Americans, the idea of proving African ancestry through genetic testing has taken on political and spiritual meaning, especially in relation to Africa as a symbol of meaning. Acquiring proof of embodied authenticity as genetically "African" can be part of a process of locating identity outside of the legacy of slavery that reduced African bodies to objects for the white master, oftentimes through the mechanism of biological classification. Within slavery, African bodies were stripped of their connection to the African continent and any other characteristic that would deem the "black race" as diverse within itself or as having any meaning outside its status as captive. Slave traders often made no distinctions between bodies from different geographical regions across the continent. Nor did they care about other markers of difference such as language or culture. "Black" signified a single racial identity, reduced to a dehumanized object that was devoid of history, culture, and rationality. Against this historical objectification, many view the genetic sciences as providing new tools through which to challenge this legacy. Genetics purportedly affirms in the most embodied way possible that one really does have a history outside of the legacy of slavery, an embodied connection to ancestors, lands, and cultures that make them so much more than objects for a white master. Henry Louis Gates Jr., one of the most prominent figures in the popularization of genetic testing for African Americans as a mode of identity construction, views genetic testing as an incredibly powerful tool for rewriting the history of African American identity. As he says in the final episode of his 2006 public television series *African American Lives*, "for the first time in three centuries we can begin to reverse the middle passage" (cited in Roberts 2011b, 232). This is quite an astonishing claim, based on the idea that knowledge of the genetic "truth" of bodies has the power to alter history and redeem the past.

This idea has certainly found its way into the imagination of many African Americans, creating a new site for the construction of complex subjectivity. Encountering the genetic reality of one's body can be understood as a religious experience leading to religious conversion. The physical makeup of bodies serves as a potential well of religious meaning. For example, on the "testimonials" page of the website for "African Ancestry", a company that does DNA screening for "people of African descent", African American pastor Kenneth Edward Copeland says this about his genetic screening results:

> The entire African Ancestry experience moved me in ways that I cannot adequately express in words. The unveiling of my ancestral connections ranks right up there with witnessing the birth of my children, the difference was that I was the one being (re)born. If you don't know your history you can't trace the trajectory of God's plan for your life and His plan for your family. God bless you African Ancestry.[3]

Copeland's testimony is consistent with many other voices on the site. Here, the terrain of religion is not, as addressed in other chapters, how the body moves, gestures, eats, or is adorned, but is in fact the very body itself, where the search for complex subjectivity is a search for meaning *within* the body. While Copeland's testimony speaks of a general experience of being "reborn", another testimony on the site from @ChicNSmart (taken from the social media platform Twitter) is more explicit in terms of redemption from the history of slavery: "The moment @AfricanAncestry reveals the tribe, so beautiful! Like snatching the family legacy back from the slave owner and those tears you shed when you find out, you finally know where home is."[4] Both testimonials display a kind of conversion narrative, where screening results function as a revelation that fundamentally changes the subject's embodied sense of history and being in the world.

Pinn provides three aspects of religious conversion, offering a helpful framework for understanding these testimonials: "1) the confrontation by historical identity, often presented in terms of existential pain and some type of terror; 2) wrestling with the old consciousness and the possibility of regeneration [...] and 3) embrace of new consciousness and new modes of behavior affecting relationship with the community of believers" (Pinn 2003, 159). Both Copeland and @ChicNSmart display all three in their testimonies. What is distinct in their cases is that the conversions occur out of a scientifically conditioned encounter *with their own bodily genetic makeup* that was once "other" and unknown. The subjects are confronted with a previously unknown historical identity (their specific African "ancestral connection" or "tribe") that has been hidden all along in their very bodies. Copeland embraces this new identity given in the genetic profile as part of God's plan for him and his family's life. He proclaims that he has finally unlocked the God-given truth of his body, and this truth has profound implications for his and other's future. For @ChicNSmart, the trauma and terror of an enslaved past is confronted, and the possibility of regeneration is realized through the genetic profile's affirmation of a true "home" outside the legacy of slavery. The use of the word "home" suggests belonging, acceptance, and comfort. The discovery of the subject's most fundamental level of physicality has moved her from a place of precariousness to a place of belonging. The subject has found the "true" historical community to which she rightfully belongs. No one can challenge this as it is written into her very body. Encountering the genetic reality of her own body—infused with historical, cultural, and spiritual meaning—a new future entailing "the recognition of a new direction for life, a new sense of self" becomes possible (Pinn 2003, 162).

The experience of discovering a genetic African identity can be linked to history of religions scholar Charles Long's emphasis on Africa as historical reality and religious image for black religion (Long 1986, 188). Despite the loss of specific African practices and cultural material, there remains a "soft culture" of African retentions. Long notes that "slaves did not confront America with a religious tabula rasa. If not the content of culture, a characteristic mode of orienting and perceiving reality has probably persisted" (p. 189). This points to the persistence of African *style* among the descendants of the Africans that bears a trace of their primordial human identity. In this way, the image of Africa has played an enormous part in the development of African American religion(s) (p. 190). Such an image does not necessarily need to be connected with the actual African continent, but rather becomes related to a narrative of the historical beginnings of black folks, *the* primordial religious image of great significance. Africa became an image through which "natural and ordinary gestures of the blacks were and could be authenticated" (p. 190).

While Long focuses on the cultural memory of Africa as a symbol of meaning, the two examples discussed above show that "Africa" also functions symbolically as an *embodied* reality that makes possible religious encounters at the level of an individual's own body. Following Long, we suggest the encounter with the bodily "secrets" that genetics unlock can function as a kind of *mysterium tremendum*, which Long, drawing from Rudolph Otto, defines as "that experience which establishes the *otherness* and mystery of the holy" (p. 151, emphasis original). For Long, this experience is an essential element in the establishment of the religious. The *mysterium tremendum* connects directly to the numinous presence of something utterly outside the rational self that evokes a religious experience within human beings, the realization of a "creature-consciousness" as Otto puts it (1958, 10). Emphasizing the "wild and demonic forms" that such an experience of otherness can take, Long suggests that it is "especially the *mysterium tremendum* that evokes our feelings of creatureliness, of the diminution of our planes and hopes; it is this feeling that leads to [...] a sense of the overpowering reality of that which stands over against us, and the fundamental distinction between the human and the divine" (Long 1986, 176). In other words, it is the experience of a total otherness to the self, a mystery that cannot be absorbed into rational understanding of the world, that provides human beings with a knowledge of their singularity in the face of an-other.

Long emphasizes that for African Americans the *mysterium tremendum* has not historically been directly associated with the sociological situation of slavery, but rather with human beings recognizing their creatureliness and their humanity before God (p. 178). And yet, the sociological situation of slavery—the situation of external oppression—"colors [...] and creates a screen [...] gives a sense of being 'born with a veil'" (p. 178). Related directly to W. E. B. Du Bois's description of African American's experience of "double consciousness", slavery "creates" an African body as a slave through a "second creation" that conceals the "first creation" of their humanity. While African Americans know themselves as fully human, the sociological situation of slavery and its broader effects mean that such humanity is always put into question. The experience of the *mysterium tremendum* names the encounter with their first creation as human beings, a discovery of the original and primordial reality of humanity written into every body. Speaking of Du Bois's experience of the *mysterium tremendum* in his encounter with a black church revival, Long describes Du Bois as "[pondering] the beauty and sorrow of his community, and these ruminations rush his consciousness back to the African forest, to the sense of a premordium of history and imagination" (Long 1986, 177). For Long, being "rushed back" to a consciousness of Africa, a land signified as an-other reality from that of the racist America in which he lives, signals the discovery of and encounter with this "first creation".

The discovery also functions as a critique of the imposed objectification to which Du Bois is subjected. The "second creation" of an imposed identity creates a myth out of the hegemony of the oppressors. The myth is simultaneously true and fictive. The truthful aspect of the myth is that there is actual, concrete oppression happening. One cannot deny the truth of a whip that is actually tearing one's flesh or being denied by law from drinking from a certain water fountain. However, the myth of the oppressor's mastery is fundamentally fictive because the oppressed know that the master's claim on them is a false, second creation. What all of this boils down to for Long is the signification of a new form of humanity no longer based on the master-slave dialectic:

> [T]he [*mysterium tremendum*] in the religions of the oppressed is the negation of the image of the oppressor and the discovery of the first creation. It is thus the negation that is found in community and seeks its expression in more authentic forms of community, those forms of community which are based upon the first creation, the original authenticity of all persons which precedes the master-slave dichotomy. (Long 1986, 184)

Against the backdrop of slavery and its still present legacy of the objectification of black bodies, the genetic link to Africa becomes for many African Americans irrefutable evidence of one's first creatureliness and their belonging within a broader historical, cultural, and spiritual community. Encountering a narrative of historical and cultural meaning written into the body itself affords a religious experience that enhances and shapes the sense of complex subjectivity at the level of mundane bodily existence. In this way, the contemporary scientific discourse of race provides a new terrain for thinking about religion, race, and embodiment. If Pinn is correct that the body is the "central terrain, the place of contestation for all things sociopolitical, economic, cultural, religious *and* theological" (Pinn 2010, 11, emphasis original), then knowledge of the genetic reality of the body potentially has great significance for how one makes meaning in life. Though we argue that race is a socially and politically constructed category that has no biological essence, it is important to recognize that biological notions of race still have great influence on how people perceive the intersections of race and identity. Almost two decades into the twenty-first century, genetic knowledge of the body will no doubt increasingly shape how bodies are perceived and given meaning. Within the framework of religion as the quest for complex subjectivity, genetic knowledge of the body presents itself as a potentially significant terrain of religious experience.

NOTES

1. For example, Benjamin Rush considered black skin to be an actual disease and sought to develop medical/chemical/biological means to whiten it and thereby remedy the socio-cultural pathologies it elicited (1799: 4).
2. See The Young Turks, "White Supremacist Finds out his Ancestors were Black", November 2013. Available from: https://www.youtube.com/watch?v=pLoel5EKT34 (accessed August 25, 2016).
3. African Ancestry, "See What Others are Saying about African Ancestry." Available from: http://africanancestry.com/testimonials/ (accessed March 26, 2016).
4. Ibid.

Epilogue

We have moved through traditions, engaged with cultural production, and explored the mundane. By now, the meaning of religion *and* body should be understood as entailing complex entities working on and in each other, framing each other even as they are framed. We looked for the inextricable relation between religion and bodies. What we found was an open and continual process of meaning-making—one inscribed on compound bodies, through their discursive constructions as much as their cellular or genetic composition. But no text provides the final word on an area.

One of our goals was to open up areas of inquiry and investigations as we think of "religion" and "bodies" as malleable, complex processes that are perpetually changing. The compound body that emerged in various ways throughout the text speaks to the body's framing of and being framed by power relations and discourses; the weight of stereotypical framings or the interrogation of the political dimension of the body through artistic expression are just two examples. If Judith Butler (1993, 2015) is correct in her assertion that the very framing of the body (indeed the body itself) is tethered to a sense of selfhood—and that this very selfhood speaks to political realities—then one could easily see how bodies and religion (again, understood as a process of meaning-making) are implicated in the way in which power operates. Or it might be possible for one to turn to the public dimensions of this connection. For instance, one could explore the public display of dead black bodies at the hand of the state. After all, Michael Brown's body did lie in the street for four hours; and, via social media, videos of black bodies in pain or in death often "go viral", speaking to what might be understood as a fetishistic voyeurism, a collective thirst for images of mangled and broken black bodies. We might hear echoes of Saidiya Hartman's (1997) analysis of Frederick Douglass' *Autobiography* wherein she refuses to recount Aunt Hester's beating; she found the very replaying of these "scenes of subjection" to do just as much damage as the acts constituting them.

While in these pages we have offered only a few examples of the intersection between religion and bodies, it is our hope that this text will open black religious studies to new and different ways of exploring the meaning of black religion, and push to develop more expansive ways of thinking about black religion in relation to the bodies that have, over time, come to be known as "black".

Bibliography

Allah, Wakeel. 2009. *In the Name of Allah: A History of Clarence 13X and the Five Percenters*. Atlanta: A-Team.
Anderson, E.N. 2005. *Everyone Eats: Understanding Food and Culture*. New York: New York University Press.
Baer, Hans and Merrill Singer. 1992. *African-American Religion in the Twentieth Century: Varieties of Protest and Accommodation*. Knoxville, TN: University of Tennessee Press.
Baldwin, James. 1962. "The Creative Process." In *Creative America*, edited by John F. Kennedy, et al. New York: Ridge Press. http://thenewschoolhistory.org/wp-content/uploads/2014/08/Baldwin-Creative-Process.pdf
Balibar, Etienne. 1991. "Is there a Neo-Racism?" In *Race, Nation, Class: Ambiguous Identities*, edited by Etienne Balibar and Immanuel Maurice Wallerstein, 17–36. New York: Verso.
Beckford, Robert. 2009. "Black Suit Matters: Faith, Politics, and Representation in the Religious Documentary." In *Black Religion and Aesthetics: Religious Thought and Life in Africa and the African Diaspora*, edited by Anthony B. Pinn, 135–52. New York: Palgrave Macmillan. https://doi.org/10.1057/9780230622944_8
Belasco, Warren James. 2006. *Appetite for Change: How the Counterculture Took on the Food Industry*. 2nd edn. Ithaca, NY: Cornell University Press.
Belting, Hans. 2011. *An Anthropology of Images: Picture, Medium, Body*. Princeton, NJ: Princeton University Press.
Berger, Peter L. 1990. *The Sacred Canopy: Elements of a Sociological Theory of Religion*. Reprint edition. New York: Anchor.
Berger, Peter and Thomas Luckmann. 1967. *The Social Construction of Reality: A Treatise in the Sociology of Knowledge*. New York: Anchor.
Bhabha, Homi K. 2004. *The Location of Culture*. New York: Routledge
Bliss, Catherine. 2012. *Race Decoded*. Stanford, CA: Stanford University Press.
Blumenbach, Johann Friedrich. 1999 [1975]. "On the Natural Variety of Humankind." In *Slavery, Abolition, and Emancipation in the British Romantic Period, Vol. 8*, edited by Peter J. Kitson and Debbie Lee, 143–212. London: Pickering and Chatto.
Bogle, Donald. 2001. *Toms, Coons, Mulattos, Mammies, and Bucks: An Interpretive History of Blacks in American Cinema*. 4th edn. New York: Continuum.
Bonilla-Silva, Eduardo. 2009. *Racism without Racists: Colorblind Racism and the Persistence of Racial Inequality in America*. Lanham, MD: Rowman and Littlefield.
Branch, Carol D. 2010. *Variegated Roots: The Foundations of Stepping*. In *African American Fraternities and Sororities: The Legacy and the Vision*, edited by Tamara L. Brown,

Gregory S. Parks and Clarenda M. Phillips, 315–41. Lexington, KY: University Press of Kentucky.

Brooks, Daphne. 2006. *Bodies in Dissent: Spectacular Performances of Race and Freedom, 1850-1910.* Durham, NC: Duke University Press.

Buchhart, Dieter. 2010. "Jean-Michel Basquiat: A Revolutionary Caught Between Everyday Knowledge and Myth." In *Basquiat*, edited by Dieter Buchhart and Sam Keller, ix–xvii. Ostfildern: Hatje Cantz.

— 2015. "Basquiat's Notebooks: Words and Knowledge, Scratched and Sampled." In *Basquiat: The Unknown Notebooks*, edited by Dieter Buchart and Tricia Bloom, 27–48. New York: Brooklyn Museum/Skira Rizzoli Publications.

Butler, Judith. 1990. *Gender Trouble: Feminism and the Subversion of Identity.* New York: Routledge.

— 1993. *Bodies that Matter: On the Discursive Limits of Sex.* New York: Routledge.

— 2015. *Senses of the Subject.* New York: Fordham University Press.

Butler, Octavia E. 2007. "*Wild Seed*" (1980). In *Seed to Harvest*, 1–253. New York: Grand Central.

Camus, Albert. 1991. "The Myth of Sisyphus." In Albert Camus, *The Myth of Sisyphus and Other Essays*, 1–138. New York: Vintage International.

Cannon, Katie Geneva. 1998. *Katie's Canon: Womanism and the Soul of the Black Community.* New York: Bloomsbury Academic.

— 2006. *Black Womanist Ethics.* Eugene, OR: Wipf & Stock.

Chireau, Yvonne. 2003. *Black Magic: Religion and the African American Conjuring Tradition.* Berkeley: University of California. https://doi.org/10.1525/california/9780520209879.001.0001

Cobb, Jelani, 2015. "Black Like Her." *The New Yorker.* June 2015. http://www.newyorker.com/news/daily-comment/rachel-dolezal-black-like-her (accessed August 15, 2015).

Collins, Patricia Hill. 2000. *Black Feminist Thought: Knowledge, Consciousness, and the Politics of Empowerment.* 2nd edn. New York: Routledge.

Copeland, M. Shawn. 2008. *Enfleshing Freedom: Body, Race and Being.* New York: Fortress Press.

Curry, Colleen. 2013. "Smithsonian Eyes Trayvon Martin Hoodie for Museum Exhibit." *ABC News*, August 2013. http://abcnews.go.com/US/smithsonian-eyes-trayvon-martin-hoodie-museum-exhibit/story?id=19836962 (accessed March 3, 2017).

Daily Mail Online. 2016. "'Racist' Cartoon Compares 'Butch' Michelle Obama to Melania Trump." *Daily Mail*, May 14, 2016. http://www.dailymail.co.uk/news/article-3590830/Fury-racist-cartoon-comparing-butch-masculine-Michelle-Obama-pageant-ready-Melania-Trump.html (accessed July 5, 2016).

Danto, Arthur C. 1997. *After the End of Art: Contemporary Art and the Pale of History.* Princeton, NJ: Princeton University Press.

Davenport, Charles. 1928. "Do Races Differ in Mental Capacity?" (Lecture, March 1928). Charles B. Davenport Papers. Philadelphia: American Philosophical Society Library.

Davies, Brian (ed.) 2000. *Philosophy of Religion: An Introduction and Anthology.* Oxford: Oxford University Press.

Deleuze, Gilles. 1969. *The Logic of Sense.* Reprinted 1990. New York: Columbia University Press.

Descartes, René. 2000. "Fifth Meditation." In *Philosophy of Religion: An Introduction and Anthology*, edited by Brian Davies, 327–9. Oxford: Oxford University Press.
Divine, Father. [1942] 1974a. "Give Thanks and Praise Every Day." *The New Day*, November 1974: 3. Reprint of a sermon given on November 26, 1942.
— 1946. "My Marriage is to Propagate Virtue, Honesty, Brotherhood and Democracy." The Peace Mission Movement, August 1946. http://www.libertynet.org/fdipmm/worddrtv/46082120.html (accessed March 12, 2015).
— 1951. "We Believe that Americanism is the Amalgamation of all Nations." October 1951. http://www.libertynet.org/fdipmm/mdbook/ameritx.html (accessed June 2, 2016).
— 1965. "The Union of God and Man." Reprint from *The New Day*, April 1965. http://www.libertynet.org/fdipmm/word2/65041020.html (accessed August 15, 2015).
— 1974b. "The Miracle of Good Health." *The New Day*, November 1974: 11–15.
— 1976. "The Rosebud Bride of the Lamb." *The New Day*, April 1976: 21.
Divine, Mother. 1982. *The Peace Mission Movement*. Philadelphia: Imperial Press, Inc.
Douglas, Kelly Brown. 1999. *Sexuality and the Black Church: A Womanist Perspective*. Maryknoll, NY: Orbis Books.
— 2005. *What's Faith Got to Do with It: Black Bodies/Christian Souls*. Maryknoll, NY: Orbis Books.
— 2015. *Stand Your Ground: Black Bodies and the Justice of God*. Maryknoll, NY: Orbis Books.
Douglas, Mary. 1973. *Natural Symbols: Explorations in Cosmology*. New York: Pantheon Books.
Drew, Ain. 2009. "Being a Sistah at PETA." In *Sistah Vegan: Black Female Vegans Speak on Food, Identity, Health, and Society*, edited by A. Breeze Harper, 61–4. New York: Lantern Books.
Du Bois, W. E. B. 1997. *The Souls of Black Folk*. Edited by David W. Blight & Robert Gooding-Williams. Boston, MA: Bedford/St. Martin's.
Duchamp, L. Timmel. 2013. "'Sun Woman' or 'Wild Seed'? How a Young Feminist Writer Found Alternatives to White Bourgeois Narrative Models in the Early Novels of Octavia Butler." In *Strange Matings: Science Fiction, Feminism, African American Voices, and Octavia E. Butler*, edited by Rebecca Holden and Nesi Shawl, 82–94. Seattle: Aqueduct.
Dyczewska, Agnieszka. 2008. "Vegetarianism as an Example of Dispersed Religiosity." *Implicit Religion* 11.2: 111–25. https://doi.org/10.1558/imre.v11i2.111
Edwards, Korie L. 2008. *The Elusive Dream: The Power of Race in Interracial Churches*. New York: Oxford University Press. https://doi.org/10.1093/acprof:oso/9780195314243.001.0001
Elam, Michele. 2011. *The Souls of Mixed Folk: Race, Politics, and Aesthetics in the New Millennium*. Berkeley, CA: Stanford University Press.
Fanon, Frantz. 1967. *Black Skin, White Masks*, trans. Charles Lam Markmann. New York: Grove Press.
Father Divine's International Peace Mission Movement [no date]. "The Lily-buds' Creeds." http://peacemission.info/mission/creeds/the-lily-buds-creeds/ (accessed April 25, 2014).
Field, Allyson, Jan-Christopher Horak, and Jacqueline Stewart. 2015. "Introduction: Emancipating the Image—The L.A. Rebellion of Black Filmmakers." In *L.A. Rebellion:*

Creating a New Black Cinema, edited by Allyson Field, Jan-Christopher Horak and Jacqueline Stewart, 1–54. Oakland, CA: University of California Press.

Fine, Elizabeth. 2003. *Soulstepping: African American Step Shows*. Urbana, IL: University of Illinois Press.

Fleetwood, Nicole. 2011. *Troubling Vision: Performance, Visuality and Blackness*. Chicago, IL: University of Chicago Press.

Floyd, Samuel A. 1995. *The Power of Black Music: Interpreting Its History from Africa to the United States*. New York: Oxford University Press.

Gordon, Lewis. 1994. "Existential Dynamics of Theorizing Black Invisibility." In *Existence in Black: An Anthology of Black Existential Philosophy*, edited by Lewis Gordon, 69–78. New York: Routledge.

Gregory, Dick. 1974. *Dick Gregory's Natural Diet for Folks Who Eat: Cookin' with Mother Nature*. Edited by James R. McGraw. New York: Harper & Row.

Griffith, R. Marie. 2001. "Body Salvation: New Thought, Father Divine, and the Feast of Material Pleasures." *Religion and American Culture: A Journal of Interpretation* 11.2: 119–53.

Grosz, Elizabeth. 2011. *Becoming Undone: Darwinian Reflections on Life, Politics, and Art*. Durham, NC: Duke University Press. https://doi.org/10.1215/9780822394433

Halberstam, Judith. 2004. "Female Masculinity." In *Literary Theory: An Anthology*, 2nd edn, edited by Michael Ryan and Julie Rivkin, 935–57. Malden, MA: Blackwell.

Hartman, Saidiya. 1997. *Scenes of Subjection: Terror, Slavery, and Self-Making in Nineteenth-century America*. Oxford: Oxford University Press

Heidegger, Martin. 2002. *Identity and Difference*. Translated from German by Joan Stambaugh. Chicago, IL: University of Chicago Press.

Heyes, Cressida J. 2006. "Changing Race, Changing Sex: The Ethics of Self-Transformation." *Journal of Social Philosophy* 37.2 (Summer 2006): 266–82. https://doi.org/10.1111/j.1467-9833.2006.00332.x

Hoban, Phoebe. 1998. *Basquiat: A Quick Killing in Art*. New York: Penguin Books.

Hopkins, Dwight N. 1999. *Down, Up, and Over: Slave Religion and Black Theology*. Minneapolis, MN: Fortress Press.

Ifateyo, Ajowa. 2009. "Journey to Veganism." In *Sistah Vegan: Black Female Vegans Speak on Food, Identity, Health, and Society*, edited by A. Breeze Harper, 110–22. New York: Lantern Books.

Jay Z. 2013. *Magna Carta, Holy Grail*. New York: Roc-a-fella records.

Johnson, E. Patrick. 2003. *Appropriating Blackness: Performance and the Politics of Authenticity*. Durham, NC: Duke University Press. https://doi.org/10.1215/9780822385103

Kahan, Benjamin. 2009. "The Other Harlem Renaissance: Father Divine, Celibate Economics, and the Making of Black Sexuality." *Arizona Quarterly: A Journal of American Literature, Culture, and Theory* 65.4: 37–61.

Kaiser, Susan B. and Sarah Rebolloso McCullough. 2010. "Entangling the Fashion Subject through the African Diaspora: From Not to (K)not in Fashion Theory." *Fashion Theory* 14.3: 361–86. https://doi.org/10.2752/175174110X12712411520331

Kant, Immanuel. 2000. "Critique of Pure Reason." In *Philosophy of Religion: An Introduction and Anthology*, edited by Brian Davies, 337–41. Oxford: Oxford University Press.

Kaplan, Carla, 2015. "Rachel Dolezal and Racial Illogic." *Chronicle of Higher Education* 61.40 http://www.chronicle.com/article/What-the-1920s-Tell-Us-About/231037 (accessed July 10, 2015).

Kelsey, Colleen. 2012. "Leos Carax, Motorized." *Interview* magazine. http://www.interviewmagazine.com/film/leos-carax-holy-motors/ (accessed 21 May 2016).

Kertess, Klaus. 1993. "Brushes with Beatitude." In *Jean-Michel Basquiat*, edited by Richard Marshall, 50–59. New York: Whitney Museum/Harry N. Abrams, Inc.

Knight, Michael Muhammad. 2007. *The Five Percenters.* New York: Vintage.

— 2011. *Why I Am a Five Percenter.* London: Penguin Books.

Kroeber, Alfred L. 1963. *Anthropology: Biology and Race.* New York: Harcourt Brace and Word.

Lennard, Natasha, 2012. "Occupiers March for Trayvon Martin at 'Million Hoodie March'." *Salon*, March 22, 2012. http://www.salon.com/2012/03/22/occupiers_march_for_trayvon_martin_at_million_hoodie_march/ (accessed August 15, 2015).

Lincoln, C. Eric and Lawrence H. Mamiya (eds.). 1990. *The Black Church in the African American Experience.* Durham, NC: Duke University Press.

Long, Charles H. 1986. *Significations: Signs, Symbols, and Images in the Interpretation of Religion.* 2nd edn. Aurora, CO: Davis Group Publishers.

Loyd-Page, Michelle R. 2009. "Thinking and Eating at the Same Time: Reflections of a Sistah Vegan." In *Sistah Vegan: Black Female Vegans Speak on Food, Identity, Health, and Society*, edited by A. Breeze Harper, 1–7. New York: Lantern Books.

Lyotard, Jean-Francois. 1984. *The Postmodern Condition: A Report on Knowledge.* Minneapolis, MN: University of Minnesota Press.

Madison, D. Soyini. 2014. "Foreword." In *Black Performance Theory*, edited by Thomas F. DeFrantz and Anita Gonzalez, viii–ix. Durham, NC: Duke University Press.

Marshall, Richard. 1993. "Repelling Ghosts." In *Jean-Michel Basquiat*, edited by Richard Marshall, 15–27. New York: Whitney Museum/Harry N. Abrams, Inc.

Martin, Michael T. 2014. "Conversation with Ava DuVernay—A Call to Action: Organizing Principles of an Activist Cinematic Practice." *Black Camera* 6.1: 57–91. https://doi.org/10.2979/blackcamera.6.1.57

Mayer, Marc. 2005. "Basquiat in History." In *Basquiat*, edited by Marc Mayer, 41–57. New York: Merrell.

McCoy, Marcella. 1998. "African American Fraternities and Sororities and African Communities: Cultural Parallels among Selected Public Rituals." PhD dissertation, Bowling Green State University.

Meadows, Tashee. 2009. "Because They Matter." In *Sistah Vegan: Black Female Vegans Speak on Food, Identity, Health, and Society*, edited by A. Breeze Harper, 150–54. New York: Lantern Books.

Miller, Monica L. 2009. *Slaves to Fashion: Black Dandyism and the Styling of Black Diasporic Identity.* Durham, NC: Duke University Press.

Miyakawa, Felicia. 2005. *Five Percenter Rap: God Hop's Music, Message, and Black Muslim Mission.* Bloomington, IN: Indiana University Press.

Morrison, Toni. 1987. *Beloved.* 1st edition. Collectible First Editions. New York: Alfred A. Knopf.

Nguyen, Mimi Thi, 2015. "The Hoodie as Sign, Screen, Expectation, and Force." *Signs* 40.4 (Summer 2015): 791–816. https://doi.org/10.1086/680326

Nuruddin, Yusuf. 1994. "The Five Percenters. A Teenage Nation of Gods and Earths." In *Muslim Communities in North America*, edited by Yvonne Yazbeck Haddad and Jane I. Smith, 109–31. Albany: SUNY Press.

Nyong'o, Tavia. 2009. *The Amalgamation Waltz: Race, Performance, and the Ruses of Memory*. Minneapolis, MN: University of Minnesota Press.

Olson, Carl. 2008. "Celibacy and the Human Body: An Introduction." In *Celibacy and Religious Traditions*, edited by Carl Olson, 3–20. Oxford: Oxford University Press.

Otto, Rudolph. 1958. *The Idea of the Holy*. Oxford: Oxford University Press.

Peace Mission movement [no date, a]. "Concept of Marriage." The Peace Mission Movement. http://www.libertynet.org/fdipmm/mdbook/marriatx.html (accessed April 11, 2016).

Pew Research Center. 2012. "How Blogs, Twitter and Mainstream Media Have Handled the Trayvon Martin Case." Pew Research Center: Journalism and Media Staff, March 30, 2012. http://www.journalism.org/2012/03/30/special-report-how-blogs-twitter-and-mainstream-media-have-handled-trayvon-m/ (accessed August 24, 2016).

Phillips, Layli. 2009. "Veganism and Ecowomanism." In *Sistah Vegan: Black Female Vegans Speak on Food, Identity, Health, and Society*, edited by A. Breeze Harper, 8–19. New York: Lantern Books.

Pinn, Anthony B. 2003. *Terror and Triumph: The Nature of Black Religion*. Minneapolis, MN: Augsburg Fortress Press.

— 2009. "Introduction: The Black Labyrinth, Aesthetics, and Black Religion." In *Black Religion and Aesthetics: Religious Thought and Life in Africa and the African Diaspora*, edited by Anthony B. Pinn, 1–18. New York: Palgrave MacMillan. https://doi.org/10.1057/9780230622944_1

— 2010. *Embodiment and the New Shape of Black Theological Thought*. New York: New York University Press.

— 2012. *The End of God-Talk: An African American Humanist Theology*. New York: Oxford University Press.

Posey, Sandra M. 2010. "The Body Art of Brotherhood." In *African American Fraternities and Sororities: The Legacy and the Vision*, edited by Tamara L. Brown, Gregory S. Parks and Clarenda M. Phillips, 269–93. Lexington, KY: University Press of Kentucky.

Powell, Richard. 1997. *Black Art and Culture in the 20th Century*. New York: Thames and Hudson.

Primiano, Leonard Norman. 2009. "'The Consciousness of God's Presence Will Keep You Well, Healthy Happy, and Singing': The Tradition of Innovation in the Music of Father Divine's Peace Mission Movement." In *The New Black Gods: Arthur Huff Fauset and the Study of African American Religions*, edited by Edward E. Curtis, IV and Danielle Brune, 91–115. Bloomington, IN: Indiana University Press.

— 2015. "The Complexion of God: The Vernacular Photography of Father Divine's Peace Mission Movement." Paper presented at Annual Meeting of the American Academy of Religion (AAR) in Atlanta, Georgia, November 2015.

Raboteau, Albert J. 2004. *Slave Religion: The "Invisible Institution" in the Antebellum South*. Updated edn. New York: Oxford University Press.

Roberts, Dorothy E. 2011a. "Collateral Consequences, Genetic Surveillance, and the New Biopolitics of Race." *Faculty Scholarship*. Paper 437. http://scholarship.law.upenn.edu/faculty_scholarship/437

— 2011b. *Fatal Invention: How Science, Politics, and Big Business Re-Create Race in the Twenty-first Century.* New York: The New Press.
Rush, Benjamin. 1799. "Observations Intended to Favour a Supposition that the Black Color (as It is Called) of the Negroes is Derived from the Leprosy." *Transactions of the American Philosophical Society* 4. https://archive.org/details/jstor-1005108 . https://doi.org/10.2307/1005108
Saggese, Jordana Moore. 2014. *Reading Basquiat: Exploring Ambivalence in American Art.* Berkeley, CA: University of California Press.
Samuels, Allison. 2015. "Rachel Dolezal's True Lies." *Vanity Fair*, July 19, 2015. http://www.vanityfair.com/news/2015/07/rachel-dolezal-new-interview-pictures-exclusive (accessed August 15, 2015).
Santosa, Melissa. 2009. "Identity, Freedom, and Veganism." In *Sistah Vegan: Black Female Vegans Speak on Food, Identity, Health, and Society*, edited by A. Breeze Harper, 73–7. New York: Lantern Books.
Satter, Beryl. 1996. "Marcus Garvey, Father Divine and the Gender Politics of Race Difference and Race Neutrality." *American Quarterly* 48.1: 43–76. http://www.jstor.org/stable/30041521 . https://doi.org/10.1353/aq.1996.0001
Sexton, Jared. 2008. *Amalgamation Schemes: Antiblackness and the Critique of Multiracialism.* Minneapolis, MN: University of Minnesota Press.
Sheppard, Samantha. 2015. "Bruising Moments: Affect and the L.A. Rebellion." In *L.A. Rebellion: Creating a New Black Cinema*, edited by Allyson Field, Jan-Christopher Horak and Jacqueline Stewart, 225–50. Oakland, CA: University of California Press.
Smith, Murray. 2010. "Dawin and the Directors: Film, Emotion and the Face in the Age of Evolution." In *Evolution, Literature and Film: A Reader*, edited by Brian Boyd, Joseph Carroll and Jonathan Gottschall, 258–69. New York: Columbia University Press.
Smith, Valerie (ed.). 1997. *Representing Blackness: Issues in Film and Video.* New Brunswick, NJ: Rutgers University Press.
Spillers, Hortense. 1987. "Mama's Baby, Papa's Maybe: An American Grammar Book." *Diacritics* 17.2: 65–81. https://doi.org/10.2307/464747
St. Anselm. 2000. "Proslogion." In *Philosophy of Religion: An Introduction and Anthology*, edited by Brian Davies, 311–12. Oxford: Oxford University Press.
Taylor, Diana. 2003. *The Archive and the Repertoire: Performing Cultural Memory in the Americas.* Durham, NC: Duke University Press. https://doi.org/10.1215/9780822385318
Taylor, Robert J., Linda M. Chatters and Jeff Levin (eds.). 2003. *Religion in the Lives of African Americans: Social, Psychological, and Health Perspectives.* Thousand Oaks, CA: SAGE Publications
The New School. 2011. "Remixed and Remastered-Part 2: Ava DuVernay." https://www.youtube.com/watch?v=aiglFyOj65A (accessed 1 June 2016).
Thompson, Robert Farris. 1992. "Royalty, Heroism, and the Streets: The Art of Jean-Michel Basquiat." In *Jean-Michel Basquiat*, edited by Richard Marshall, 28–43. New York: Harry N. Abrams, Inc./Whitney Museum of American Art.
— 1993. *Face of the Gods: Art and Altars of Africa and the African Americas.* New York: Prestel.
— 2011. *Aesthetic of the Cool: Afro-Atlantic Art and Music.* Pittsburgh, NY: Periscope.
Torbeson, Craig. 2010. "The Origin and Evolution of College Fraternities and Sororities." In *African American Fraternities and Sororities: The Legacy and the Vision*, edited by

Tamara L. Brown, Gregory S. Parks and Clarenda M. Phillips, 37–66. Lexington, KY: University Press of Kentucky.

Townes, Emilie. 2006. *Womanist Ethics and the Cultural Production of Evil*. New York: Palgrave Macmillan. https://doi.org/10.1057/9780230601628

"Trayvon Martin Update: Story is Now More Covered than Presidential Race." *Tampa Bay Times*, March 30, 2012. http://www.tampabay.com/blogs/media/content/trayvon-martin-update-story-now-more-covered-presidential-race (accessed August 15, 2015).

Turman, Eboni Marshall. 2014. *Toward a Womanist Ethic of Incarnation: Black Bodies, the Black Church and the Council of Chalcedon*. New York: Palgrave MacMillan.

Tuttle, Will. 2004. *World Peace Diet: Eating for Spiritual Health and Social Harmony*. New York: Lantern Books.

United Nations General Assembly. 1963. Preamble. http://www.un-documents.net/a18r1904.htm

Valentine, Sarah. 2013. "The Divine Auditor." *Prairie Schooner* 87.2. http://www.prairieschooner.unl.edu/?q=excerpt/divine-auditor (accessed August 15, 2015).

— 2015. "When I Was White." *Chronicle of Higher Education* 61.40. http://chronicle.com/article/When-I-Was-White/231347 (accessed July 10, 2015).

Walker, Alice. 1983. *In Search Of Our Mothers' Gardens—Womanist Prose*. San Diego, CA: Harvest/Hbj.

Wallace, Michele. 1999. *Black Macho and the Myth of the Superwoman*. New York: Verso Books.

Washington, Harriet A. 2008. *Medical Apartheid: The Dark History of Medical Experimentation on Black Americans from Colonial Times to the Present*. New York: Harlem Moon.

Watts, Jill. 1992. *God, Harlem, U.S.A.: The Father Divine Story*. Berkeley, CA: University of California Press.

Weiss, Gail. 1999. *Body Images: Embodiment as Intercorporeality*. New York: Routledge.

Wemple, Erik, 2013. "Fox News's Bill O'Reilly Blames Trayvon Martin's Death on Hoodie." *Washington Post*, September 16, 2013. https://www.washingtonpost.com/blogs/erik-wemple/wp/2013/09/16/fox-newss-bill-oreilly-blames-trayvon-martins-death-on-hoodie/ (accessed August 15, 2015).

Williams, Delores S. 1993. *Sisters in the Wilderness: The Challenge of Womanist God-Talk*. Anniversary edition. Maryknoll, NY: Orbis Books.

Witt, Doris. 2004. *Black Hunger: Soul Food and America*. Minneapolis, MN: University of Minnesota Press.

Wolters, Raymond. 1975. *The New Negro on Campus: Black College Rebellions of the 1920s*. Princeton, NJ: Princeton University Press.

Wright, Richard. 2007 [1946]. *Black Boy: A Record of Childhood and Youth*. New York: Harper Perennial Modern Classics.

Young, Harvey. 2010. *Embodying Black Experience: Stillness, Critical Memory, and the Black Body*. Ann Arbor, MI: University of Michigan Press. https://doi.org/10.3998/mpub.235634

Young, Robert. 2001. *Postcolonialism: An Historical Introduction*. Malden, MA: Blackwell.

Index

African American Film Releasing
    Movement (AFFRM) 72–3
agency 52, 67, 69, 75, 83, 101, 103
Allah (Clarence 13X) 33–6, 39–41, 121
ALLAH (Arm, Leg, Leg, Arm, Head) 32, 34,
    37, 40
Anselm of Canterbury 38–9
Aquinas, Thomas 37

Baldwin, James 60
Basquiat, Jean-Michel 47
    and graffiti 51
    and *Gray's Anatomy* 51
    and hip hop culture 54
    and inverted/exposed bodies 52–6
    and Jack Johnson 52
Beckford, Robert 114
Beloved (Morrison) 60, 66–9
Belting, Hans 48–9
BGLOs (Black Greek Letter
    Organizations)
    and black religion 92
    and bodily aesthetics 86–7
    and branding and stepping 87–92
    and meaning-making 87–92
    and the social body 83–4, 87
    formation of 84–6
black representation 3, 5, 10n.1, 59, 62,
    64, 73, 114
    and cinematic objectification 71, 75
    in Peace Mission Movement 26, 28
    in visual art 47, 50, 56–7
    "positive" and "negative" images
        72, 81
    social significance in cinema 73

black women
    and cultural tropes 62–3, 69, 76
    and resistance 60, 65, 76
    as complex subjects 69, 72, 76
    representations of 59
Blaxploitation film 71, 73
Bless Their Little Hearts (Woodberry) 74
Bliss, Catherine 129–30
Blumenbach, Johann Friedrich 126
bodies
    and aesthetics 51, 86–7
    and branding 87–90
    and complex subjectivity 83–6
    and cultural worlds 53, 56–7
    and emotive performance 74, 77
    and fashion/dress 98–102, 112–13
    and Greek social life 84–6
    and narrative cinema 71
    and performance studies 25–8
    and photography 16, 27
    and race/racism and 3, 8, 99–100
    and sexuality 3
    and the social body 83–4, 87
    and stepping 90–2
    as site of religious struggle 1
    bodily symbolism 88–90
    compound 3–4, 24, 48, 50–51, 54,
        71, 98
    corporeal schema *see under* Fanon,
        Frantz
    discursive 3–5, 7, 9–10, 10n.1, 24,
        49, 75, 101
    hybrid 14, 22, 24, 26–9, 29n.2
    of the enslaved 68
    material 3–5, 48, 53

reconstruction of through art
images 48–50, 53, 58
branding
and bodily symbolism 88
and identity 87–90
and personal meaning-making
88–90
Brooks, Daphne
and spectacular opacity 76
Buchart, Dieter 53–4
Butler, Judith 25, 137
Butler, Octavia E. 59, 64 *see also Wild Seed*

Camus, Albert 54, 58n.1
Cannon, Katie G. 60, 62, 67, 127
capitalism
and agricultural production 118–20
celibacy
discursive body and 20, 24
heteronormativity and 28–9
in Peace Mission Movement 13–14,
19–25, 28–9
material body and 23–4
post-racial 28–9
Chireau, Yvonne 10n.2
Clarence 13X *see* Allah
Cobb, Craig 131–2
Cobb, Jelani 110
Collins, Patricia Hill 62–3, 78
complex subjectivity
and art/aesthetics 57–8, 114
and embodied emotion 79–80
and everyday life 2–3, 106–7,
114–15, 118, 125
and Five Percenters 40, 42
and identity 2–3, 59, 61, 63, 111–13
and meaning-making 57, 61, 82,
86, 131
and religious conversion 112, 132–3
and rituals of reference 2
and social relations 80
and womanism 60–1
black religious traditions and 1–3,
27
compound body and 3–4

cultural production and 2–3, 47, 59,
69, 72, 75–7
definition of 2–3
discursive body and 3–4
in cinema 75
in Peace Mission Movement 27
material body and 3–4, 118, 125,
132–3, 136
ontological possibilities 2–3, 27, 59,
83, 106, 109, 115
performance of 27
Copeland, Kenneth Edward 133
Copeland, M. Shawn 9, 10n.1

Danto, Arthur 47–9
Davenport, Charles 127
Descartes, René 38–9
Divine, Father 16
as God 13, 16–17
marriage to Mother Divine 13–14,
21–2
see also Divine, Mother; Peace
Mission Movement
Divine, Mother
marriage to Father Divine 13
reincarnation and 21–2
virginity of 13
see also Divine, Father; Peace
Mission Movement
Dolezal, Rachel 6, 98, 107–11, 131
Douglas, Kelly Brown 9–10n.1, 116n.2
Douglas, Mary
and complex subjectivity 83
and embodiment/bodies 3, 84, 86
dress
and criminality 100, 104–6
and everyday religion 97, 101, 106,
113–15
and gender and sexuality 98–9, 103,
107
and material/discursive embodiment 98, 102, 114–15
and race/racism 99–101, 103–6,
110–1, 114
and respectability politics 105

interpretations of dressed bodies 102, 105–6, 108, 114
social norms of 98–9, 108
see also fashion subjectivity
Du Bois, W. E. B. 135
Duchamp, L. Timmel 65
DuVernay, Ava 72–3, 79

Earths (Five Percenters) 32, 34–7, 40, 42
Elam, Michele 26
embodiment see bodies

Fanon, Frantz 6, 39, 99–103, 109, 115
corporeal schema 99
historico-racial schema 99, 105
racial-epidermal schema 100, 102–3, 109
fashion see dress
fashion subjectivity 100–2, 106, 109, 113–15
and complex subjectivity 101, 106, 113–15
and racial identity 109, 113
Fillmore, Charles 21
Five Percent Nation
and "science" 40
and "show and prove" 40
Flexible (Basquiat) 47, 53–4, 56–7
food
and cultural identity 117
codes and rituals for 117, 121
see also soul food; veganism
Forward Movement 72–3

Garner, Margaret 66–7
Garrison, Ben 59, 62
Garvey, Marcus 19
Gates Jr., Henry Louis 132
gender
and bodies 3
norms of 35, 63–4, 69, 98–9
performance of 5, 14, 63–4, 69
see also transgender identity
genetics
and ancestor tracing 132–6

and diversity of the human species 129
and surveillance 130
see also race and biological classification
god
and Five Percenters 32–7, 39–42
Father Divine as 16–17
in philosophy of religion 37–9
Mystery God 34
Gordon, Lewis 39
Greek fraternities and sororities 84–5, 87
see also BGLOs (Black Greek Letter Organizations)
Gregory, Dick 122–3
Griffith, R. Marie 17, 23–4
Grillo (Basquiat) 47, 54–7

Halberstam, Judith 63
Heidegger, Martin 34, 39, 41
Historically Black Colleges and Universities (HBCUs) 82, 86, 92
Human Genome Project 125, 129
hybridity
in Peace Mission Movement 14, 22, 24, 26–9, 29n.2
see also interraciality; post-raciality; race-neutrality

interraciality
in Peace Mission Movement 16, 18, 25
see also hybridity; post-raciality; race-neutrality
Islam
as acronym (I, Self, Lord, And, Master) 34, 40
see also Nation of Islam (NOI)

Jenner, Caitlyn 107–8

Kahan, Benjamin 20, 24
Kaiser, Susan 100–1, 113
see also fashion subjectivity
Kant, Immanuel 39

Kaplan, Carla 109–10
Kroeber, Alfred 127

Lee, Spike
    School Daze 82, 89–90
Long, Charles
    Africa as symbol of meaning 134
    and interdisciplinary scholarship 10n.2
    mysterium tremendum 134–6
    religion as orientation 2
    signification 8
Los Angeles Rebellion 73–4
Los Angeles School of Black Filmmakers 73–4

Martin, Trayvon 6, 102–7, 109
McCullough, Sarah 100–1, 113
    see also fashion subjectivity
meaning-making
    and BGLOs 86–91
    and branding 87–90
    and religion 82, 86
    and stepping 90–2
Mendel, Gregor 126
Miller, Monica L. 101
Miu Miu ("Women's Tales" film series) 75
Morrison, Toni 59, 66
mother nature 122
Muhammad, Elijah 41, 121
    see also Nation of Islam (NOI)

Nation of Gods and Earths *see* Five Percent Nation
Nation of Islam (NOI) 33–5, 39–40, 121
neo-racism 128
New Day (periodical) 14, 23
    see also Peace Mission Movement
New Thought 17, 19, 21–2, 24

ontological proof (for God's existence) 33, 36–42
ontology 2–3, 6, 27, 54, 57, 59, 101, 110, 112

Peace Mission Movement 13
    celibacy in 13–14, 19–25, 28–9
    Crusaders 19–20
    food practices and 23–4
    gender and 14
    hybridity in 14, 22, 24, 26–9, 29n.2
    Lily-buds 19–20
    mainstream American ideals and 14, 17–18, 29
    New Thought and 17, 19, 21–2, 24
    photography in 14, 17–19, 22, 24–7
    physical immortality and 23–4
    race-neutral/post-racial performances and 16, 18–19, 22, 25–7, 30n. 4
    reincarnation 13, 21
    Rosebuds 19–21
    segregation and 27
    use of racial categories 17, 25, 30n.10
    virginity 13, 20–1
    see also Divine, Father; Divine, Mother
Peninnah 21–3, 30n.9
    see also Divine, Father; Peace Mission Movement
phenomenology 38–40
philosophy of religion 32–3, 37, 42
photography
    in Peace Mission Movement 14, 18, 22, 24–7
Pinn, Anthony B. 2–4, 63, 75, 79, 83, 106, 112–13, 133, 136
    and the body as place of contestation 136
    Black Religion and Aesthetics 114
    see also complex subjectivity
post-raciality
    in Peace Mission Movement 16, 18, 28, 30n.4
    see also hybridity; interraciality; race-neutrality
predominantly white institutions (PWIs) 85
Primiano, Leonard Norman 22, 26

race
- and biological classification 126–30
- and culture 128
- and Peace Mission Movement 16, 18
- constructionist vs essentialist theories of 107, 109
- racial "passing" 108–9
- transracial identity 108, 111–12, 116n.3
- *see also* neo-racism

race films 73
race-neutrality
- in Peace Mission Movement 26

reincarnation 13, 21
Ritchings, Edna Rose *see* Divine, Mother
Roberts, Dorothy 129–30

Satter, Beryl 14, 17–9
Sheppard, Samantha
- and black emotional interiority 73–4
- and cinematic bruising moments 77

Smith, Murray 76–7
Smith, Valerie 71–2
soul food 120–2

stepping
- and body symbolism 90
- and circles and strolls 91–2
- as communal meaning-making 90–2

Townes, Emilie M. 9–10n.1
transgender identity 107–8, 116n.3, 116n.4
- and fashion/dress 107
- and race 108

transubstantiation 104
Turman, Eboni Marshall 9–10n.1

United Nations 128

Valentine, Sarah 111–13
veganism 118, 120–1, 123
visual art
- and politics 47–9

Walker, Alice 60–2, 66, 69
Washington, Harriet 130
Wild Seed (Butler) 60, 64–5
womanism 10n.1, 60–2, 68
Woodberry, Billy 74
Wright, Richard
- *Black Boy* 117–18

www.ingramcontent.com/pod-product-compliance
Lightning Source LLC
Chambersburg PA
CBHW071849230426
43671CB00012B/2119